Studying Creative Writing—Successfully

Edited by Stephanie Vanderslice

Imprint Information and Credits

ISBN: 978-1-907076-86-2(Softback edition)
978-1-907076-87-9 (ePub edition)
978-1-907076-88-6 (PDF edition)

Published under the Creative Writing Studies imprint
by Frontinus Ltd
Registered office: Suite 7, Lyndon House, 8 King's Court,
Willie Snaith Road, Newmarket, Suffolk, CB8 7SG, UK

Publisher's website: http://pandhp.com
First published 2016
© Stephanie Vanderslice and contributors

Credits
Cover image: Rika Newcombe (www.rikanewcombe.co.uk)
Cover design, text design and typesetting: Benn Linfield
    (www.bennlinfield.com)
Development editing: Hannah Strawson
Copy-editing: Karen Haynes
Index: Christina Garbutt
Proofreading: Will Dady
Printed by Lightning Source and Printondemand-worldwide

Disclaimer

Frontinus Ltd has no responsibility for the persistence or accuracy of URLs for external or third-party websites referred to in this publication, and does not guarantee that any content on such websites is, or will remain, accurate or appropriate.

The material contained in this publication is provided in good faith as general guidance. The advice and strategies contained herein may not be suitable for every situation. No liability can be accepted by Frontinus Ltd for any liability, loss, risk, or damage which is incurred as a consequence, whether direct or indirect, of using or applying any of the contents of this book or the advice or guidance contained therein.

The publisher and the author make no warranties or representations with respect to the completeness or accuracy of the contents of this work and specifically disclaim all warranties, including without limitation warranties of fitness for a particular purpose. No warranty may be created or extended by sales or promotional materials.

Copyright: Rights Deals and Permissions

To acquire rights, including translation rights, or permission to reproduce text, please contact our rights manager via info@frontinus.org.uk.

Series Information

Studying Creative Writing—Successfully is the seventh title to be published in the international series, Creative Writing Studies. The series comprises titles on creative writing designed for use—by scholars, students, and teachers—in higher education settings.

The first six titles in the series are:
Rethinking Creative Writing in Higher Education
   by Stephanie Vanderslice
Teaching Creative Writing: Practical Approaches
   edited by Elaine Walker
Creative Writing: Writers on Writing
   edited by Amal Chatterjee
Studying Creative Writing
   edited by Sharon Norris
Caves of Making
   by Philip Gross
Researching Creative Writing
   by Jen Webb

Contents

Editor's Preface

If you are holding this book in your hands, you are probably one of several audiences we envisioned for it. You may be considering becoming, or just starting out as, a creative writing student at a university or college, and wondering what this course of study is all about, how to proceed and where it can take you. Or, you may be considering graduate study in creative writing and, coming from another undergraduate major, may be wondering how studying creative writing in higher education works and how you can get yourself caught up before you enter your program. This book is also for you. Or, you may be studying creative writing at an advanced level but have always been perplexed by some of what seem to be the unspoken practices of the field. It's always good to have a firm grasp of the rationales and purposes behind the signature habits of a discipline. Studying creative writing, or any subject, at advanced level means you may encounter rules and procedures that might seem bewildering. The authors of the essays in this book want to demystify the subject for you.

In fact, the authors of this book probably remember what it was like when they were making their way through the creative writing landscape for the first time, and wish they'd had a book like this to guide them. Between them they have had well over a hundred years of experience in teaching and studying the subject. They want to share that knowledge and experience to clear a path for you. Enjoy your journey.

STEPHANIE VANDERSLICE

Acknowledgements

As always, my family, especially John Vanderslice, are the inspiration that makes all my work possible. In addition, I wish to thank the University of Central Arkansas for granting me the sabbatical leave period that gave me time to work on this book, and to express my appreciation to all the contributors for being such a pleasure to work with and for making this such a valuable resource for students studying creative writing in North America today. Finally, I owe a great debt to Hannah Strawson for her keen editorial eye and to Karen and Anthony Haynes for an editorial vision that has done so much to advance the cause of creative writing theory and pedagogy.

Chapter One

Making the Creative Writing Major Work for You: Planning Now for the Best Outcome

STEPHANIE VANDERSLICE

There are lots of good reasons to become a creative writing major: because you love to read, because you love to write, because you have a rich imagination, because you love words, because you like to use your creativity to solve problems. You'll notice, however, that those listed do not include: because you want to support yourself solely as a writer or become the next J.K. Rowling or Stephen King. That's because it's practically impossible to support yourself solely as a writer, only 0.05 percent of writers ever achieve that goal, and creative writing programs would be selling you a bill of goods if they told you that this was likely. In fact, right now, four students who have graduated from our undergraduate creative writing program are publishing books—really excellent books—and we are justly proud of them, but none of them support themselves through advances or sales on these books. Becoming a writer is a long apprenticeship, one that requires years of patience. Once you do become a published writer, the financial rewards take a long time to accrue to the point that you may be able to support yourself through your writing. The happy news, however, is that any creative writing major worth its salt, which is most of them, is already preparing you for many careers that will sustain people who enjoy

1

working with words while they are also developing as writers and artists.

Here's another bit of news, however. Once you've declared yourself a creative writing major, the years will pass quickly. And the time it takes to prepare for a career that will sustain you after you graduate requires careful planning that needs to begin soon after you've made your commitment to the major. Otherwise, you might find yourself on the eve of graduation in a panic thinking, "Now what?"

Our program boasts a long list of gainfully and happily employed graduates for two main reasons: 1. A creative writing program teaches certain skills and habits of mind that are useful in the workforce and 2. These students dedicated themselves to making the most of what they had learned to find employment after they graduated. Let's look at the kinds of skills you acquire with a degree in creative writing and how you can engage them throughout the pursuit of your degree.

First, the obvious. You are a strong writer, and that is an ability held quite dear in today's workplace. Most people are daunted by the idea of writing a paragraph. That's nothing for you. You write a short story in an evening. You are not intimidated by the written word—a quality that's hard to come by today. This is something you need to emphasize at every opportunity when you seek employment, something we'll talk about later. Second, you know that strong writing always involves revision and you're good at that, between all the workshopping, peer review and revision you do as part of your coursework. Revision is also something others are not always willing to do to create a strong product, but it's something you know all about. Finally, through workshopping, peer review and the writing process itself, you've learned how to use writing and creative thinking to solve problems and this is a skill that can be adapted to many careers.

Possible Career Paths for Writing Majors

If you're someone who loves the world of reading and writing, however, chances are you don't want to work in just *any* field. You want to work in a field that is in some way allied with the writing arts, you want to spend your days working with words. Fortunately, with a little planning, that's more than possible. Our graduates enjoy fulfilling jobs in a long list of writing-related fields, such as: magazine and book editing and publishing, technical writing, web content developing, literary agenting, social media and book publicity, librarianship and teaching K–university. For the most part, however, these positions didn't just happen. By and large, the students who have been most successful in securing fulfilling positions after they graduated were the ones who started thinking about and planning it almost from the moment they declared their major. Perhaps even before. On the other hand, the students who have the most difficulty are the ones who realize during the last semester of college that, oh my gosh, they are going to graduate and have to get a JOB! What will they do? These are the kinds of students who often end up under-employed after they graduate, because they haven't been doing the kinds of things during college that would prepare them for life afterwards.

How Can I Plan My Creative Writing Major To Benefit Me Later?

EARLY ON: EXPERIMENT

Early in your college career, you have time to experiment and figure out what you like to do and what you're good at, as well as what you *don't* like to do. Take advantage of it. Try different genres. Sure, maybe you've written fiction since you were seven, but you'll never know if there is a hidden poet or dramatist inside you if you don't try those courses. Believe me, I've seen enough poets turned fiction writers or fiction writers turned poets after one course in sophomore year that I cannot recommend this kind of experimentation strongly enough. Besides, every genre in creative writing teaches you something about the other ones—so the techniques we learn in poetry inform our fiction and vice versa. What have you got to lose? Everything, if there's a voice inside of you that never gets heard.

While you're trying different genres, try different subjects in writing as well. Take that class in editing, technical writing or digital writing. For example, I've often seen many a student discover she has a "gift" for writing in digital formats that she never knew she had until she exercised it in our department's Writing as Information Design course. Courses such as these will also broaden your skillset, always an advantage in the post-college workforce.

Experiment when it comes to extracurricular activities too. Working on the college literary magazine is an obvious choice, as is working for the newspaper and even the yearbook. All of these publications show you know how to work with text and images and layout software and how to work with others as a team. Try not to spread yourself too thin, but also consider trying a few other activities that might support your interest in reading and writing. Perhaps there's a group that reads to kids at the local Boys and Girls Club or book club that promotes speculative fiction. Give it a try.

THE MIDDLE YEARS PART I: <u>GET AN INTERNSHIP</u>

Internships, short-term work experiences in a field you want to enter, are critical; I cannot emphasize them enough. If you do not do internships while you are in college, you will be doing them when you are out. Internships are often—but not always—unpaid positions where you learn about the dimensions of a particular job, say, literary agenting or magazine production, in exchange for your labor. Our graduates have completed a long list of productive internships, such as working for a national literary magazine (the *Oxford American*), doing web design for a local catalog business, writing for a national nonprofit (Heifer Project International) and working for a local magazine, just to name a representative few. There is some controversy around internships, especially around the fact that most graduates need at least one (and often more than one) to get an entry-level position these days—that's a lot of free labor going around and it gives a special advantage to upper middle class students and beyond who can afford to take some time to work without pay. But controversy aside, I don't see them going away anytime soon. They're a fact of life. If you can persuade your family to support you for a few months while you do one, and if you can live at home or with friends or relatives, that's best. But in fact, there are ways you can do an internship and paid work at the same time. You can do an internship part time and earn part time, perhaps even only ten hours a week. These days, you can even do an internship offsite, online. Yes, you'll be working hard, but it will only be for a few months and the long-term benefits will be worth it. You get the idea. If you're flexible and creative, which you know you are because you're a creative writing major, you can figure something out.

But what are the long-term benefits of an internship? What can it do for you? Well, truthfully, the benefits are many, but the first might be finding out if a type of work is *not* for you. I have seen many students enthusiastically sign up for, say, an editing internship, only to discover by the internship's end that, wow, they really hate editing. It's really good to find this out before you spend four years cultivating the kind of experiences designed to suit you for a career in editing and publishing when you'd be happier doing something else, like information design. Internships also introduce you to the world of work, give you valuable hands-on skills you may not be able to learn in class and access to real-world experience and equipment you also may not be able to get in class. They also help you build the web of networks you will need to tap into to find a position when you graduate. The best kinds of internships are those that can get you college credit, so that at least if you're not getting paid, you're moving a step closer to your degree.

How Do I Get an Internship?
Internships have become so common that most departments have set up a coordinator to handle them, so that is usually the first person you should go to as he will usually have the lowdown on the best internships and how to get credit for them. Often, the Office of Career Services on your campus also coordinates internships. Failing that, you can set up your own internship and meet with your department chair to see about finding a way to get credit through an independent study.

Lots of program directors tell me that they have trouble getting students to understand the value of an internship.

For this reason, some programs have gone so far as to make the internship a requirement of their programs and I can see why. Students who attend my university often work at least part time and it's hard to get them to see the benefits, no, the necessity of taking on extra work (though if they're doing it for course credit, they can at least take one less course). But the truth is, doing a degree without doing an internship is truly the "old school" way of looking at your university education and that's "so twentieth century." It really won't get you anywhere.

The Middle Years Part II: Be Teachable

One of the qualities I've noticed in my more successful students, that is, the ones who are able to develop more quickly as writers and to adapt better to life post-graduation is that they were more teachable. What do I mean by that? Well, they had a more flexible mindset, one that was open to what their professors had to teach them. Not that they were little drones, drinking up everything their professors poured down their throats and then spitting it out on tests, à la Pink Floyd, but that they took everything in from all their professors, turned it over and over in their minds, considering it, and deciding, after much deliberation, what was worth keeping. Unfortunately, I've encountered a fair number of students, maybe 20–25 percent, who seem to have already made up their minds about the world and believe and treat the rest of their educational experiences as a vehicle for a. proving how much they already know and b. attending to only what is presented to them that supports their narrow worldview.

What saddens me most about these students is how much they are limiting themselves. Universities work fairly hard to assemble a diverse faculty. Our department alone, for example, boasts faculty with close to one hundred years of education and experience in the literary world to share with its students. For whatever reason, however, some students are not open to this range of education and experience; they don't particularly want to soak up all that is available to them. They resist the suggestions we offer, even though they are only that: suggestions. Nothing is more frustrating to a teacher. We want to help; we want to mentor; we want to give students the benefit of all we have learned. We only ask that they listen with an open mind; in part, because that is what pleases us as teachers and in part because, as teachers, we've watched many students move through our classes and out into the world and it's the teachable ones who seem to do better in the long run. It's the less teachable ones who end up giving up on their creative writing hopes after a year (sometimes less) or two for a more "practical" and easily obtainable but less fulfilling line of work. Meanwhile the more flexible, teachable ones are able to apply the many, many lessons they've learned along the way from an array of different teachers to building a satisfying work/writing life for themselves.

We want that for you.

THE FINAL YEARS PART I: GET ANOTHER INTERNSHIP
Seriously. I'm not kidding. It won't hurt and it can only help. Scratch most post-grads happily settling into their first position and you'll find not one, but two internships. Three would not be unheard of. Besides, sometimes that second or third internship leads directly into…you guessed it: the first paying, post-graduate job. You don't want to pass that up, do you?

THE FINAL YEARS PART II: GRADUATE SCHOOL

Some of our most serious writers- or literary-editors-to-be really want to go on to graduate school for an MFA (Master of Fine Arts, which is usually a studio or practically-based advanced degree in writing) or for an MA (a Master of Arts, usually in literature with a creative concentration), sometimes as a stepping-stone to a PhD. In fact, sometimes, the MFA is not only a great stepping-stone to a writing career but also to a career as an editor or an agent or writing teacher. So if you're serious about any of these, you do want to consider graduate school. Considering an MFA doesn't mean you don't need to do any of the activities I have mentioned before, however, and in fact, all of them, including internships, extracurricular activities and being teachable, will only make you more attractive to graduate programs. Moreover, you must be cautioned against considering graduate school, especially an MFA, *only* because senior year is rolling around and you're not sure what else to do with your degree. Getting into an MFA program at this point will likely be difficult and you may incur a lot of debt—and you don't want to do that.

Honestly, a lot of graduate schools, ours included, like to see students with a couple of years of work and adult life experience under their belts before they pursue an advanced degree, so if you want to try out a post-undergrad job for a year or two before heading back for an MFA, most will encourage it. But if you're chomping at the bit to continue with what you already know you want to do, here is my advice: early in the process, get yourself a copy of *The Creative Writing MFA Handbook, Second Edition* by Tom Kealey and read it from cover to cover.

Read it again, marking it up where it pertains to you. Then do what the book says, again, where it pertains to you. I advise many of my undergrads on getting an MFA but I won't even talk to them until they've read this book.

THE FINAL YEARS PART III: BE PATIENT
Okay, so you did everything I told you to do, every single thing and it's been two months since graduation and: nothing. No interviews. No bites. Here's what you need to know. This might take a little time. But it will happen. If you've done everything in this chapter, I can pretty much promise you it will.

Finding a job in a creative field is not the same as finding a position in accounting, for example—something you will be very grateful about when you are not chained to your cubicle in the months leading to tax time, when, in fact, you are not chained to a cubicle at all. That's because this field is not as vocational; it's not a matter of plugging X candidate into Y spot. It's a much more complicated matter than that. It takes more time. It could take three months. It could take six months. It could take a year or more. I've never seen it take more than two—unless the job seeker has some pretty high salary expectations to start out. But hang in there—pick up some part-time work on the side, lower your expenses, live with family if you can, don't go out and acquire a car payment yet. Getting a foothold is usually all you need in the arts to stay in and start moving up. Don't give up too soon.

THE END IS JUST THE BEGINNING: SUCCESS STORIES
What kind of credibility would I have if I didn't share some student stories with you, to give you an idea of how

you might plan your journey. Here goes (names have been changed for the sake of confidentiality).

Joanna

Joanna had returned to college a bit later in life with two middle-school children and a husband but she had a lot of fire and determination about writing. She roamed widely among the different courses offered in the creative writing major, availing herself of as many as she could, including digital writing courses in our general writing major. She also wrote novels and kept a blog and worked in the university writing center, where she mentored younger students and made a big impression on the faculty. As graduation neared, Joanna realized that her family limited her mobility for graduate school but it didn't dampen her passion for literature and writing. She applied for a position directing a small library in her hometown nearby, and due to the high regard of her professors and the positions of responsibility she'd held as a student, she got it. While director, she spearheaded many youth programs, often creative-writing-based, and began studying for her Master of Library Science (MLS) online, all the while surrounded by the latest in books and continuing to work on her writing. She has now finished her MLS, works as the reference librarian for the main branch of the county library, and is still surrounded by books and still writing. And she's looking for her next challenge.

Cecilia

Cecilia was always passionate about poetry and excited that in our department, she could take so many courses in poetry and in writing in general. She took independent study courses with leading poets. She took courses in fiction and nonfiction writing to improve her poetry. She even took a course in Aspects of the Creative Life and learned how to connect to the regional and national arts communities in promoting her creative work. In her senior year, she applied to and was accepted into an MFA program in a mid-Western city. Here she worked on her poetry, interned on the program's literary review, and in very short order, with a few friends, established a poetry press that continues today to publish cutting-edge poetry and fiction. She has received many grants and awards for her own poetry and is making a name for herself in the poetry world. She loves being active and she loves dogs, so to support her poetry and her press, she works for a dog-walking company during the day. She works just enough to support herself and to support the press, which has gained a strong reputation, and to have enough time to do her own work.

Jake

Jake has been passionate about writing and reading ever since he can remember. He was also passionate about teaching; it wasn't a "fallback" career for him. He edited the college literary magazine as an undergraduate, worked as an intern for a local independent press and wrote an honors thesis on coming-out narratives that was worthy of publication in an academic journal. Jake was torn between teaching high school and college some day. He knew teaching college would be intellectually challenging but he also knew he could perhaps make the greatest difference in students' lives teaching high school. He applied to a number of MA programs in literature with a creative writing emphasis, where he thought he could write more and reflect more thoroughly on whether he wanted to teach high school or college, and had a number of good funding options to choose from. During graduate school in a top program in a nearby state, he continued writing poetry and winning awards, taught first year composition and Upward Bound and ultimately decided that what he really wanted to do was teach high school. He returned to Arkansas after he graduated with a master's degree with no student debt and has been teaching high school here for several years, still writing poetry and inspiring a love of writing and reading in his students. He teaches special units on social justice and the Holocaust, leads his classes in National Novel Writing Month, coaches the winning Quiz Bowl Team and quietly and not so quietly changes lives.

CONCLUSIONS

All of these students followed quite different paths but they all have one thing in common. They were all mindful as they pursued their education, thoughtful as they elected their creative writing degrees, consciously charting their courses. Always planning and thinking ahead, they left very little to chance, always electing courses, internships, programs and activities that, while they enjoyed them, also brought them closer to their individual goals. As a result they now lead working lives that fulfill them by intersecting closely with reading and writing, the world of words.

Chapter Two

Studying Creative Writing at Today's College or University: What Should I Expect and What Skills Should I Bring?

TRENT HERGENRADER

Before we get started, a caveat: there is no way to write a chapter that can accurately prepare you for everything to expect from your college experience, much less from an individual program such as creative writing. Our country boasts the best higher education system in the world, and this is in part due to the wide variety of experiences available to students. This chapter offers some broad advice about what to expect from studying creative writing regardless of where you find yourself taking courses, and how you can get the most out of your creative writing program.

1. When It Comes to What Constitutes "Creative Writing," Have an Open Mind

Creative writing is an umbrella term that covers all kinds of creative activity. How far that umbrella reaches depends on who you ask. No one questions that fiction and poetry are the two bedrocks of creative writing in the university, though the genre of creative nonfiction has been gaining momentum in recent years and is now a prominent feature of many creative writing programs. Even if we stick with poetry, fiction, and creative nonfiction, distinguishing between these genres can be challenging—indeed, many authors often intentionally try to conflate them. Is a

14

dense paragraph of lush, lyrical prose considered very short fiction or poetry? What, if anything, distinguishes a piece of evocative first-person journalism, a research essay written with literary flair, and autobiographical nonfiction? In high school, you may only have been exposed to work that neatly demarcates these genres, but in college you're likely to encounter work that disrupts simple notions of what constitutes a short story, what work an essay does, what forms poetry can take. Many experimental works can be frustrating or resist interpretation. You don't have to like every piece you read, but you should keep an open mind in terms of what the author might have been trying to achieve, and remember that some writers *want* their readers to struggle, hopefully in productive, mind-expanding ways. Not every piece of creative writing is meant to be entertaining.

Some creative writing programs include courses in drama and screenwriting, while other schools offer those classes in the theater and film departments. Visual and interactive media have steadily risen in popularity in recent years, as has performance poetry. From a strictly traditionalist standpoint, this can all seem very frightening as creative writing loosens from its mooring to words written on paper. Other instructors (like yours truly) view this as liberating and choose to incorporate diverse media such as graphic novels, digital poetry, interactive fiction, videogames, films, blogs, podcasts and more into the classroom. From class to class you might find yourself asking, "What is this doing in a creative writing class?" or perhaps the opposite, "Isn't there more to creative writing than this?" These are open-ended questions you are likely to revisit over your lifetime as a person interested in the literary arts. As you enter the creative writing community, avoid assuming a hardline stance as you attempt to answer them. You don't need to accept that a composite of vapid celebrity quotes constitutes a brilliant piece of "found" poetry, but at least entertain the idea. The very act of considering the claim may help you achieve some insights as to what you value as creative work and how you define it.

2. *Trust in the Process*

You will find out, if you haven't discovered it already, that writing can be a real grind. While many people believe that writers wait for divine inspiration, the truth is much more mundane. Successful writers know that you need to sit down and commit to putting words on the page, even when—perhaps *especially* when—you just don't feel like it. You're probably not going to feel like doing other things required of student writers either, including analyzing craft aspects of assigned readings, critiquing your peers' pieces, and revising your own writing. Instead of being carried away on a wave of heady creative energy, all this stuff feels suspiciously like work.

So here's a secret: it *is* work, and it's not all pleasurable. Ever heard the old saying *the journey is the reward?* Becoming a successful writer operates on a similar principle. Writers often joke about taking ten years to become an overnight success. While it's easy to daydream about achieving literary stardom, it's much harder to envision the steps it takes to get there, and harder yet to follow through on them. Learning the craft of creative writing takes time, and in addition to producing your own writing you will be expected to read published work, critique other students' writing in progress, and incorporate the critique you receive into revised drafts. It's important to understand the importance of each of these steps in your own progress as a writer and invest in the whole process, not just the parts you find to be fun.

Writing instructors often talk about the need for students to *read as writers.* This entails going beyond whether we enjoyed a given poem, essay, or story and examining specific matters of craft in an attempt to understand how a piece works. Beginning creative writing students often get hung up on what an assigned reading is supposed to *mean* rather than focusing their attention on techniques the author used. "What's the point of this poem?" is a less productive question than "why did the poet choose to break the line here?" In my experience, I note that students often resist work that denies a quick interpretation. However, the close analysis of craft usually helps us make some sense of a complex work of art. Sure, you can skim fifteen poems a few minutes before class to say you've done the reading, but you're unlikely to glean anything useful from it. If you're serious about creative writing, give the readings their due, even if they're not your proverbial cup of tea. Circle bits of language you like, jot questions in the margin, look up words you don't know. All of these practices highlight the fact that writing is a series of choices made by the author, and choices you make yourself when you're writing. By considering the choices other authors made, you'll begin to see a wider range of possibilities for your own work. Tim Mayers will discuss this much more in the next chapter.

The same advice holds for critique sessions, or the "workshop" part of creative writing where you respond to your classmates' work. Regardless of how your instructor structures your class, critique sessions rely on the good faith and hard work of the participants. You are likely to have wonderful workshop experiences. You are also likely to have a clunker or two. There's nothing as frustrating as giving a thoughtful, measured critique of a classmate's work only to receive a handful of bland, vague platitudes in return. Unfortunately, it goes with the territory. The good news is that you learn a lot by providing a good critique as it helps cement concepts about craft in your own mind, especially if you use proper terminology. For example, when responding to line breaks in a classmate's poem, refer to whether the lines are enjambed or end-stopped; committing to using the appropriate terminology not only reminds you what craft aspects you should focus on, it also allows you to provide a more succinct critique.

Incorporating the feedback you receive into revised work also presents a challenge. There's an old saying that a battle plan never survives contact with the enemy, and the same could be said about a manuscript and its audience. The natural urge is to turn criticisms back on the readers—it's their fault they didn't get what you were doing. The reality, however, is that the writer creates and develops reader expectations with each word, so it's up to you to listen to how readers reached their conclusions about your work. Yes, sometimes readers misread or misinterpret, but often a clumsy phrase or vague description caused the problem. Revision literally means "to see again," and if you're doing it honestly it means reassessing the choices you made in writing—the good and the bad—in light of your readers' responses. Take criticisms at face value, even if you don't agree with them at first. Readers may misidentify problems, but that doesn't mean they're wrong. For example, it's common for fiction readers to point out an ending that doesn't feel quite right. Upon revisiting the story, you might discover that the problem is actually *not* the ending, but rather a previous scene that inadvertently suggests a different conclusion. Other times, after reviewing your critique comments, no obvious solution presents itself. That doesn't mean you should just fix any typos and resubmit. Writing instructors expect you to make fresh decisions *and* be able to justify them, even if your solutions create new problems. Doing this kind of word-by-word, line-by-line tweaking can make you feel a million miles away from the euphoric rush you originally felt while writing, but the mistake is to think that your inability to nail it the first time means you're a failure. Quite the contrary. I recently placed a story that had been sitting on my hard drive for *six years*. Do I wish it would have been accepted sooner? Sure, but it took me a half-dozen significant revisions to find the right balance. Refusing to quit is a big part of becoming a successful writer. It's all part of the process.

3. Set Goals and Push Yourself

Creative writing talent is not distributed equally. Some people have a knack for language rhythms or storytelling that others don't, and that's okay. We teach creative writing to develop the talent that people *do* have. And, like with all college learning, it can take months or years before some piece of wisdom suddenly clicks and finally makes sense. Much of this is out of your control. Happily, you have total control over one crucial aspect of the creative writing process: effort.

If you're reading this book, it's likely that you've already had some success with your writing. That might be winning a local contest, writing for your high school paper, receiving high praise from your teachers, or perhaps you've even been published. Or it could be the case that you're just starting to take your creative writing seriously. Regardless, until you win the Nobel Prize in Literature, you've always got some higher goal to reach for—and I'd bet even Nobel Prize winners would admit to always seeking out fresh writing challenges. This is a long way of saying that your motivation to improve your writing must come from within—you've got to be willing and eager to push yourself forward. Extrinsic rewards in the form of audience praise or seeing your name in print provide an undoubted thrill, but the glow fades quickly. As you grow as a writer, you will gain greater satisfaction from having a diverse body of work rather than being a one-trick pony.

"Pushing yourself" will mean different things to different writers, and it will mean different things over the span of your writing career. For many beginning writers, working up the courage to let others read their work is a major achievement. Once you clear that hurdle, the next goal is usually trying to get something published. After being published a handful of times, some writers set a goal to see their work in print in a specific prestigious publication; others focus on trying to win a literary prize or gain recognition within a certain community of readers; some wish to build a portfolio to entice an agent who can help them land a contract with a major publishing house. In almost every writer's case, the road is long and full of setbacks, and the process moves at what can feel like an excruciatingly slow pace. Having any kind of writing career, even a part-time one, requires an abundance of patience and determination. Setting realistic goals can keep you moving forward, and

the ability to shift gears and try new things will help stave off the dreaded "writer's block."

There is no better time to experiment with your writing than in an undergraduate writing program. Experimentation can take many forms. If you're used to writing fiction from a first-person perspective, try writing from the third or even second person; if you normally write about characters who are similar to you, write from different points of view—swap genders, races, social classes, ages. Try on different hats. Rest assured, your readers will let you know what you got wrong. Listen and learn. You might never choose to write a story from that perspective again, but the feedback can identify weak points in your writing. This experience helps you create more well-rounded characters, and thus write better, more engaging fiction. If you write free verse, challenge yourself to experiment with a variety of poetic forms; if you tend to write abstract, imagistic poems, try writing a narratively-driven prose poem; if your inclination is to write long, make an effort to write something very short. While you might have fewer outright successes when you experiment with new approaches, your work will be stronger for it when you return to your more natural writing habitat. And who knows, you might even discover talents you didn't know you had.

Prose writers should take at least one poetry workshop and poets should take one prose workshop. Hopefully you will get exposure to multiple genres of creative writing in an introductory course, but if you don't get that experience in your program, take the initiative yourself. Approach each genre with a positive attitude. The lessons you'll learn about the evocative use of language, conciseness, structure, and more are readily portable across all the genres and to other types of writing as well.

I also encourage all of my students to experiment in different forms of media. Fascinating things can happen when we mix language with images, audio, and interactive elements, and the best part is that we don't quite know where any of this kind of writing is headed. Will social media develop its own identifiable artistic aesthetic? How will technology shape, and be shaped by, our desire to tell stories? People already say "code is poetry." How will this concept continue to evolve, or perhaps be challenged, in the coming years? These are but a few of the questions that will be answered by the next generation of writers and poets, and you will be hard-pressed to find a greater concentration of intellectuals willing to entertain such ideas than on a college campus. Of course you should spend time learning how to craft language, but be bold in the application of your newfound skills. The publishing industry is still in the midst of a sea change in terms of handling the growth of digital writing. There's no better time to be a pioneer.

4. Join (or Form) Your Local Literary Community
Earlier, I stressed the importance of sitting down and writing. The actual act of writing tends to be a solitary business, perhaps because writers tend to be excellent procrastinators. Distractions, especially in the form of other people, lure you away from the keyboard. Many writers prefer to work in isolation, turning off cell phones and having the willpower to stay off email and social media sites during a writing project. For many, it's the only way to get anything done.

Yet writing also has a social side. After all, if you're not writing for an audience, you might as well just keep a private diary. At some point we want to share our work with others, and that sharing has many potential outlets. Soliciting feedback from a critique group is one of the earliest forms of sharing, and submitting work for publication is an attempt to reach a wider audience. Others present their work orally at reading series, open mic nights, literary festivals, and poetry slams. Still others join online communities and post their work for feedback, or self-publish using blogs or videos. In fact, when you decide you want to share your work, you might find yourself paralyzed by options. A good way to solve this is to start at home, so to speak, and join your local literary community.

Literary communities come in all shapes and sizes, with members joining and dropping out all the time. One great benefit of being on a college campus is that you're likely to find multiple literary communities, including those sanctioned or organized by the creative writing program. These communities commonly include an extracurricular creative writing club, a reading series, and a literary magazine. Membership tends to be informal and people often belong to multiple groups. Whether or not you participate in a group will depend on what you wish to get from it, and ultimately if it meets those needs. Those looking for shrewd critique of their work won't appreciate a more casual, social group who like to talk about what exciting things they're reading. Still, finding writers with similar interests can be hugely beneficial, so it's worth exploring your options and understanding not everything will be a good fit.

A campus creative writing student group's goals will depend greatly on the members and the faculty advisor associated with the group. Some student groups operate as workshops outside the confines of the classroom, while others might organize social outings for students and faculty interested in creative writing. It's not uncommon for them to host their own events separate from the creative writing program. Indeed, some groups want faculty involvement in planning activities, while others want independence from such structures. Depending on the size of your school and the popularity of the program, your creative writing club may have a dozen members who meet once a semester, or one hundred students or more, complete with elected positions and an annual budget. Regardless, a creative writing club is worth looking into as you'll potentially meet some like-minded peers. Look for fliers or ask a faculty member about the student creative writing group and attend a meeting or two. Keep your personal writing goals in mind and don't be afraid to politely walk away if the group isn't meeting your needs.

Literary communities thrive on readings. They provide a chance for writers to share their work in a public space, often in an intimate setting such as a coffeehouse or bookstore, where audience members are encouraged to socialize before and/or after the presentation. They may happen on campus or somewhere nearby in the community. Most universities bring in writers to speak on a variety of topics and read from their work, and it's common for the program to reserve special time for visiting writers to meet with students. Take advantage of such opportunities! After you graduate, you are unlikely to have the chance to ask accomplished writers about their writing process, literary influences, or any other questions. It's part of what makes attending college such a unique, valuable experience.

Most campuses will also have a reading series in which you may participate. Again, these can vary widely in nature so be sure to attend a few before volunteering to read. Some will be quiet affairs with a dozen people sitting in a circle, while others pack rooms to their capacity with a raucous crowd. Often a reading series will pair a faculty member with a student, either randomly or around a theme or genre. In any case, it's a great chance to hear what kind of work your classmates and instructors are doing outside the classroom. Reading your work before a room of people can be daunting, but it gets easier with experience. It's also a great way to motivate yourself to work on a piece of writing until it's well honed.

Joining your school's literary magazine is another great way to involve yourself in the local literary culture. You'll find that putting together a decent publication takes a lot of effort. Most literary magazines are always on the hunt for assistant editors—the people who read the bulk of submissions and pass the most promising work on to the senior editors for final selections. As writers, it's easy to complain about lazy editors who reject our work with no explanation or suggestion for improvements, but working as an assistant editor gives you valuable experience on the other end of the process. You'll see much subpar work that you won't finish reading before rejecting; you'll read stories that don't get started for four pages, sag in the middle, or drag on forever; you'll see poems devoid of imagery or that include horrible rhymes; much of what you'll read will be competently written but lacking in some way, though it might be hard to put your finger on how to improve it; and then you'll find the one submission that's so visceral and exciting that it demands to be immediately reread. The process invites you to bring these observations back to an honest assessment of your own work before you submit it for publication.

Reading submissions and deciding on the content is only part of putting together a literary publication. There's choosing artwork, working on the layout, managing subscriptions and distribution, copyediting, writing editorials, communicating with advertisers, and more. All of this gives you valuable experience in addition to the lessons you glean from reading submissions. It also allows you to expand your network of contacts as you develop relationships with contributors and become familiar with publications similar to yours. Normally you will need to volunteer for a semester or two before you'll be eligible for any senior positions, but then you will have more say in the aesthetic and editorial direction of the publication. The more work you put in, the greater the sense of ownership and pride you'll feel when it reaches your readers, and it can be a greatly rewarding experience.

5. *Bring a Good Attitude and Have Fun*

Another time-honored bit of lore regarding creative writing has to do with the writer as tortured genius. Moody, brooding, and petulant, she has no time for the inconsequential work of her peers as she struggles with her inner demons few can understand. He spends time wallowing in depression, booze, drugs and bad relationships that fuel the raw truth he bleeds on the page, giving future biographers plenty of juicy gossip to sink their teeth into.

Yeah, right.

Okay, there is *some* chance that writing will vault you to superstardom and worldwide acclaim, but the odds are not good. That doesn't mean you can't have a successful career as a writer, but it might mean expanding how you define success. Very few people earn a livable wage from creative writing pursuits alone; many, many more support themselves by teaching, working in publishing, or even having a career that has nothing to do with the arts and they simply write on the side. Of the handful of writers I know who do draw a hefty annual salary based on their bestselling novels, it took them years—decades, even—before making their breakthrough. All of them freely admit that in the fickle world of publishing, their writing could go out of vogue and their income would drop to zero overnight. As a result, they all live rather modest lifestyles in unglamorous places in Ohio or Colorado, not New York City or Montreal. They do not party with rock stars. They do have families and drive sensible cars.

Why mention this? To encourage you to approach your creative writing as a very *low stakes* endeavor. Don't misunderstand me: I'm not saying to treat your writing as unimportant. You should definitely take your writing seriously and produce work you can be proud of, but you want to avoid at all costs putting yourself in a position where your emotional or financial health rests on the quick acceptance of your writing. Popular TV shows and movies tend to understate the challenges—particularly the financial stress—of trying to scratch out an existence as a professional writer in a major metropolitan city. You can't make rent in Manhattan writing poetry, even if you're the voice of your generation. This isn't to suggest you should live a cloistered lifestyle. By all means, move somewhere new and exciting on a shoestring budget, travel as far and wide as you can, and generally live life to its fullest; your writing will be better for it. Just don't expect creative work to fund it, at least not initially.

The opposite approach—that is, treating your writing as a *high stakes* endeavor—usually results in anxiety and then writer's block, both of which are highly counterproductive. You don't need to be the best writer in your program, win a prestigious contest, or land a story in *The New Yorker* to be a "real" writer; you just need to keep writing. Even if you're one of the more talented writers in your program, be sure to check your ego. Swelled heads and prickly opinions erode a literary community, forcing people into rival camps where the backbiting and sniping replace actual writing. It might all feel very dramatic at the time, but treating your classmates as rivals needlessly creates a poisonous atmosphere.

So relax. Have fun. Enjoy playing with language. Take risks, try new things, and avoid petty feuds. Be positive. In your writing career you will, in turns, feel like a literary genius and a complete fraud. Rest easy knowing neither is really the case and don't be discouraged. Any pressure you feel to produce as a writer will be self-inflicted, so head this off by maintaining manageable expectations. If you're not sure what those expectations should be, speak with your professors. They can be excellent judges as to whether some technical limitations are holding you back, or whether some prompts or experimental techniques might help you out of a rut. If you're not enjoying writing, mention that as well. Suffering for your art is a choice, and rarely a very good one.

And Now: Onward!

In summary, it's pretty simple: have an open mind, try new things, become engaged, have fun. The remaining chapters in this book go into more specific details on each area. A golden rule of the creative writing workshop applies here: when people seem to be saying similar things, pay attention. They're probably onto something!

Chapter Three

Reading as a Writer, Writing as a Reader

TIM MAYERS

If you have expressed an interest in studying creative writing, it is likely that somewhere along the line, someone has told you that in order to be a great writer you must also be an avid reader. Perhaps it has even been suggested to you—either explicitly or implicitly—that you must be a great reader *before* you can become a great writer. Let's get that particular idea out of the way first: if you want to be a writer, then write. Don't wait around until you think you've read "enough" that you're finally ready to begin writing; that way, you run the risk of never actually getting started as a writer. The truth is: no one can *ever* read enough. During the eighteenth century, the word "literate" didn't simply designate a person who *could* read; it designated a person who *had read*: a person who was believed to have read all of the most important things out there to be read. This was a great and noble accomplishment. And perhaps such a thing was possible in the eighteenth century, when there were far fewer books published than there are today. Perhaps such a thing was not possible even then. But it's surely not possible today. You can't read *everything*. In fact, you can't even come remotely close. But you can read a great deal. And that's exactly what you should do.

But that doesn't mean you shouldn't be writing also. If you want to learn to play the piano or the guitar, you need to start playing right away. Might it help to listen to (or watch) skilled players of those instruments as well? Of course. But you need not wait until you have listened to or watched them all before you get to playing yourself. You should be learning and practicing, and looking for examples of expertise, *at the same time*. And the same should be true of writing. As you work on, practice, and hone your skills with your own writing, you should also be reading.

Writers Read Differently

Although reading is indispensable for anyone who wishes to be a good writer, it is *not* necessarily the case that all avid readers are good writers. It matters not only *that* you read, but also *why* and *how* you read. My father was probably the most avid and dedicated reader I have ever known, usually working his way through three or four books a week, mostly spy and thriller novels or books about historical events like the Kennedy assassination or the Vietnam War. Yet my father was never a very confident or effective writer; he sometimes asked me for help when he was facing an important writing task at work, which wasn't very often. He loved *reading* novels and books about history, but he never had any desire to *write* those kinds of books—or any other kinds of books, for that matter. He frequently told me that he read only for two purposes: to be entertained or to learn new information. His reasons for reading were not the same as they would have been had he desired to write books also. His reasons for reading affected the way he read—quickly but efficiently, intent on getting to the end of the story to find out what happened (in the case of novels) or to the end of the book to absorb its most important facts and insights (in the case of history books). My father read a great deal, but he did not read like a writer, and this suited his purposes very well. But reading that way will not suit *your* purposes, if you wish to be a writer.

What does it mean, then, to read like a writer? You probably already know some of the answer already, whether you realize it or not. Reading as a writer doesn't mean that you *don't* want to be entertained or gain new information and knowledge; it means that you must do *more than that*. You probably know this on some level because it was most likely reading that got you interested in writing in the first place. There was probably some moment in your past (or perhaps a series of such moments) when you so fell in love with a story or novel or poem, when you were so emotionally or intellectually moved by what you were reading, that you thought to yourself, *I really want to be able to do that too; I want to be a writer.*

Reading as a writer means that you are interested in how other writers put things together. You will ask yourself questions like: Why did that novelist end her first chapter in that particular place? What made her choose that moment? Why did her characters act that way? Why did she use dialogue so sparingly or so extensively? Why does she describe the physical settings in her novel in so much (or so little) detail? Why do her sentences tend to be so short, or so long, or of such mixed and varying lengths? How does she keep the narrative moving along so smoothly, so that you seem—as a reader—compelled to turn the pages, compelled to keep going? Or if you are interested in writing poetry, you might ask, as you are reading: Why does the poet write in such short lines, or such long lines, or in such a mixture of line lengths? How is he able to create such evocative images while using so few words? Why do his words sound so musical when you read them out loud or "hear" them in your head? How are such poetic effects created? When you read as a writer, you should always have such questions somewhere within the realm of your attention. Sometimes they will be in the foreground, sometimes in the background, but they should always be there.

A few years ago, I attended a rock concert with a friend I first met in high school. My friend is a musician who plays several instruments but is most interested in the guitar. He got us great seats; we were only three rows from the stage, and thus only a few yards away—for most of the concert— from the band's guitarist. I do not consider myself a musician. I played the clarinet for a couple of years in elementary school, and I learned the bare-bones basics of playing the drums while in college. Soon after the concert started, I was enjoying the performance and the great seats. But I noticed that my friend, who was also clearly enjoying the show, was watching differently than I was. He was focused in like a laser on the guitarist's technique. A couple of times, he even took a small notebook out of his pocket and jotted something down. He was watching the show not only as a spectator but also *as a musician*. He was taking full advantage of his opportunity for a close-up "lesson" with a guitarist he admired. He was watching the show not only to enjoy it, but also to help himself become a better guitarist. Successful writers, in their own ways, must learn how to do the same sort of thing as they read.

Take Their Word for It

You don't simply need to take my word for it that reading is important for writers. The vast majority of successful writers, if they talk about writing or write about writing, likely say something at some point about the importance of reading. Reading provides positive models for you—those you would like to emulate, or at least try to emulate. Reading also provides negative models—those you do not want to emulate. Writing offers so many possibilities that it is necessary to see what other people have done in order to figure out what you want to do, and what you don't want to do.

One could fill an entire book—or more—with quotes and passages from successful writers about the importance of reading for writers throughout their lives. Here I will just briefly mention a couple. Stephen King neatly sums up a few important points in just a single page of his memoir *On Writing*: "One learns most clearly what not to do by reading bad prose" he states, noting that a key moment in his own development came when he read a science fiction novel he thought was really bad. He then claims that a key moment in your development as a writer will likely come when you realize that your own writing is "unquestionably better" than that of some other writer who has been published—and paid. The other side of this coin, according to King, is experiencing the writing of someone else who strikes you as better than you can ever hope to be. For writers who are eventually successful, this becomes a motivating force: "You cannot hope to sweep someone else away by the force of your writing until it has been done to you" (p. 146)

Joyce Carol Oates, in a wonderfully evocative essay called "Reading as a Writer," notes that so many successful writers acknowledge the debts they owe to other writers, writers whose work made a firm imprint on them as readers, especially in their youth. She sums up what she has learned via her own experiences, and via reading about the experiences of others, very nicely in this bit of advice: "*Read widely, read enthusiastically, be guided by instinct and not design. For if you read, you need not become a writer; but if you hope to become a writer, you must read*" (p. 110, italics in original). In many ways, the chapter you are now reading is an exploration and extension of Oates's wise and sound advice.

IMITATION OR INFLUENCE?

One of your goals as a writer is probably to be unique, to be *original*, to develop a style or a voice that people can recognize as yours and no one else's. Sometimes, this striving for originality makes developing writers concerned about what may happen to them as a result of reading. What if, they may wonder, I wind up seeming too much like the writers I am reading? What if I become so overwhelmed by the voices and styles of other writers that I seem imitative and unoriginal? What if I wind up seeming like a clone or copy of some other writer? This is a legitimate concern, but it should not stop you from reading.

The word "imitation" may have a bit of a bad reputation, but that need not be so. Publishing a story or poem that comes across as an obvious attempt to imitate some other writer may not be a good thing. But just as musicians and dancers and soccer players need practice, so too do writers. And imitation, for many writers, can be an important part of that practice. In fact, imitation has a long and prominent history in many areas of human endeavor. In ancient Greece, students who wished to become effective public speakers were often put by their teachers through long and

35

grueling rounds of imitation. By composing and delivering "practice" speeches based on the examples of prominent and accomplished orators, students learned important techniques of speechwriting and delivery; later, they could try to combine and recombine some of these techniques, creating their own "original" styles as a kind of mash-up of the styles of others. Likewise, during the Renaissance, students across Europe were encouraged to write poems in direct imitation of famous poets, on the assumption that by not only observing, but also practicing such poetic skills, they would develop their poetic "muscles," which could later be put to more original use.

You may want to try direct imitation of some of the writers you most admire. Think of this work as practice. The more writers you try to imitate, the more styles and techniques you will gain experience with, and the more options you will have available to yourself in the future. Eventually, imitation may become *influence*, which means something a bit different. Your best writing may look very different from the writing of those who have influenced you the most, but you will realize—and your readers may realize—that you would not have developed as a writer in quite the way you did without the presence of those other writers in your life.

Reading Around
All right. So we agree by now (I hope) that extensive and careful reading of other writers—especially in the genre(s) in which you aspire to write—is important. But is that enough? Probably not. If your work is to succeed with readers, you will need to know—or at least convince your readers that you know—about the things, places, activities,

and kinds of people that appear in your work. If your main character in a story is a ballet dancer, you will need to know something about ballet in order to portray your character convincingly. If one of your characters is a football coach, or a trumpet player, or a warehouse supervisor for an online bookseller, you will have to know—or *seem* to readers like you know—about those activities and occupations as well. If you write a poem set in London or New York City or a remote plains town in western Canada, you will need to know those places well enough to write about them, whether you have been there or not.

One of the oldest and perhaps most misunderstood pieces of advice doled out to aspiring writers is that you should *write about what you know.* On one level, this makes perfect sense; if you know something, you should be able to write about it better than someone who does not. But in practice, it's almost never that simple. You may know, for example, the grief of losing a parent, the pain of breaking up with someone you have loved, or the joy of witnessing the birth of a child. You may know the adrenaline rush of scoring a goal in overtime in a hockey game, or the sudden empty feeling of being the goaltender who is scored upon. But that does not mean you will necessarily be able to write about these things, effectively and evocatively, for readers. In fact, if you try to write about these things while still in the grip of the emotion they elicit, you may wind up coming across as inarticulate or not genuine. Writing, ironically, sometimes requires a certain sort of detachment from experience, a kind of distance, in order to be at its best.

Your experience, ideally, will inform your writing, but not all of your writing will flow *directly* from your experience. As noted above, you may wish to write about characters who are different from you in some important way, or about places you have never been. Sometimes, this will mean that as a creative writer, you will need to do some research. You may think of research as being associated mostly with scholarly or informational writing, but research can be important for fiction writers and poets too. If you write a story in which the main character is a police officer, you may need to do some research about police procedures. If you want to set a story in Paris, but you have never been there, you may need to do some research about the history and geography of the city. If you are writing a poem about black holes or quasars, perhaps you will have to do some research in astronomy.

So—read about things that are of immediate relevance to your own writing, certainly. But also read about things that generally interest you. You never know when some piece of knowledge or insight you have gained through reading might come in handy for a future piece of creative writing; at that moment, you may realize that you have unwittingly done some of your research in advance. But don't only read about things that currently interest you; also read in order to search for new things that *might* interest you. Read as both an observer of and a participant in the world. Read with the confidence that, as a writer, every word and every page that you read might help you someday, in expected or unexpected ways.

Chapter Four

Invention: Get Started and Keep Going

Travis Nicholson

Writers are frequently asked this question: Where do your ideas come from? Often the answer isn't a simple one. The muse rarely descends in a sudden, blinding realization of truth. A fever dream doesn't instantaneously provide a vivid, complete story. Typically creative writing is like any other inventive process in that a short story or poem doesn't spin itself into existence out of nothing. A tremendous amount of effort goes into building a solid writing project. Piece by piece, the work comes together. The problem is, how do we find those pieces?

Picture this: Thomas Edison in his Menlo Park laboratory, working tirelessly to heat a thin filament to make that first light bulb glow. Sweat beads on his forehead as he tinkers with the flow of electrical current. Now pull back a little. Bits of metal and glass lie scattered across a table. Precision tools line a workbench. Pull back further. Books, journals, and scraps of paper are stacked floor-to-ceiling in some places, each one filled to capacity with handwritten notes and observations. Hundreds of failed experiments lie in a pile of discarded waste. Suddenly a soft white light floods the room with an incandescent shine. Edison has finally had his lightbulb moment. The purpose of this chapter is to help you gather some creative building blocks of your own—in this case, your thoughts, impressions, observations, and emotions. Different strategies can be implemented to maximize your creative workflow. We will explore these different avenues of invention that will lead to a lightbulb moment of your own.

Set Up a Work Space and Routine

Before pen meets paper or fingers make that first keystroke, a writer must feel comfortable in his or her environment. For some of us, sitting in a crowded bookstore or coffee shop offers an ideal writing locale. Others may need the quiet retreat of an office or the comfort of a living room sofa. Choosing the right place to work can set the mood for focus, stamina, and creativity. Remember, Thomas Edison had his laboratory set up exactly how he wanted. So choose what is right for you.

Your writing space should serve as a dedicated location to do the bulk of your work. Writing on the go has its benefits, but the majority of the time you will be at home while working. Choose an area that you feel the most comfortable in. The décor of your space can and will have an effect on you. Keep this in mind as a visually "busy" room may either distract you or give a boost to your creativity. Personally, I need a variety of objects to look at and touch in order to think, so my office is covered with posters, art prints, action figures, and other manipulatives. In the end your writing space will be a reflection of your own personality and writing needs, so by all means set it up how you see fit.

Once you have a space to work, the next thing you should do is establish a writing schedule, a routine of sorts. If you are anything like the rest of the writing community, life will often get in the way of any set schedule. Try to be flexible, but don't put your writing at the bottom of your priority list. Choose a time of day (or night) when you are certain to have the fewest obligations. Many writers advise working in the early morning hours before the day truly begins. That way, all of your attention is on the writing, plus it feels like your project is priority number one. Set a realistic word/page count goal for each day. Even one page per day adds up to a novel-length manuscript over the course of a year.

Rid Yourself of Distractions

Now that you have a comfortable space and your favorite writing utensil, let's talk about your most valuable resource—time. There are only so many hours in the day and a typical writer has all sorts of obligations to meet. If you are serious about writing, the amount of time you spend on your project should reflect that. First of all, separating yourself from family and friends for extended periods is not what we mean when we say rid yourself of "distractions." Your personal life is more important than writing, but there still has to be a bit of balance. During your scheduled writing time, try not to pick up the phone or let anyone come over for a visit. It is your time to produce, so let others know that you will be unavailable. If you are the life of the party and can't get away from social obligations, schedule your writing time during late hours or early in the morning before everyone comes calling. We all have people in our lives who take up our valuable writing time, but our biggest enemy to time management is often ourselves. Being alone in a room for long stretches of time breeds temptation for goofing off. Common time wasters include social media, television, games, clickbait articles, etc. If you realistically cannot resist these distractions, distance yourself from them in your workspace.

The online world constantly beckons the writer to submit to its will. What starts as an open internet window for research becomes a rabbit hole of time suck from which you may never escape. So you may want to turn it off for the time you have set aside specifically for writing. It's as simple as disconnecting from your network or flipping the Wi-Fi switch to "off". Removing the internet from the equation frees up your mind from constant web browsing. This goes for the phone as well. Too often I find myself scrolling through some website on my phone instead of working, when I honestly can't remember even picking up the device in the first place. Need to do research for your project? If this is the case, do your research before you sit down to write. The amount of time you'll save by already having your information is well worth it in addition to eliminating temptation to open up that social media site.

Free Writing

Free writing is exactly what it sounds like. Just sit down and start writing. Don't overthink what you're doing. In fact, try not to think at all. Write what comes to you. Characters, settings, dynamic lines of dialog, or single vivid images are fair game for free-writing time. These things don't have to be connected to anything you are currently working on, but after you fill up a few notebook pages you may find something noteworthy that you want to use or build a new project from.

A second, and equally valuable, use for free writing is to break through bouts of writer's block. Free writing can open the floodgates and get some potentially useful ideas out on paper. Often the word or image you are looking for is simply stuck in your head. Once your project hits a wall, the level of frustration you feel hits the roof. Sitting down and writing down your stream-of-consciousness thoughts and feelings serves as a bulldozer to get your mind back on track. One helpful tip in this case is to write outside the genre on which you are currently focused. Don't clutter your mind with even more confusion about what you want to write—rather, begin writing something completely opposite. The act of writing will loosen you up and take some of the pressure off, and there is no greater motivator than seeing hundreds, if not thousands, of words on the page.

Some free-writing exercises to consider include:

- Timed writing: Set a clock for fifteen minutes and write what comes to your mind. Everything on the page at the end of that time is your original thoughts and/or feelings that have been hiding in the deepest corners.
- Prompted writing: Choose a writing prompt from a book, website or app to structure your writing around. Even though the topic is predetermined, don't overthink it. Be as serious or silly as you want to be in the moment. Try genres outside of your comfort zone for even more interesting results.
- Word association: Make a list of unusual or unique words and build images around them. This technique serves as both a free-writing activity as well as a vocabulary builder. You never know when you'll find a new favorite word.
- Image spinner: Type the name of a random person, place, or object into a search engine. Pull up the first images that are associated with the chosen name. Write a scene involving that person, set in that place, or centered on the item. The random nature of the "game" will keep you on your toes.

Keep a Journal (Dreams and Daily Life)

While free writing is the act of putting pen to paper with no endgame in mind, journaling takes a more deliberate approach to generating ideas. Journals can, but need not be, highly personal in nature. Edison kept a work journal cataloging and detailing his invention process. By the end of his life, he'd left hundreds of records, journals, and papers about his work on the light bulb and other projects. Keeping a daily journal can be one of the most rewarding endeavors a writer can undertake. Everyday life presents countless potential story ideas. Even a writer from small-town America experiences noteworthy moments on a daily basis.

There are multiple benefits to keeping a daily journal, and not all of them are strictly related to writing. First of all, you will learn to observe your surroundings. In the immortal words of Ferris Bueller, "Life moves pretty fast. If you don't stop and look around once in a while, you could miss it." Once you slow down and observe what is going on around you, story ideas will begin to formulate more easily from your own experiences. Places you go, activities you participate in, events you witness, and most importantly, people you meet are all wells to draw inspiration from. Keeping a record of these things makes it easier for you to recall and draw from later in the process. In the end, writing is a craft based on life. Even the most experimental work relies on some semblance of verisimilitude for an audience to find it at all relatable.

Dream journaling can be a helpful tool as well. How often do you wake up in the middle of the night from the most incredibly vivid dream, just to have it slip through your fingers the next morning when you try to remember the details? Keeping a notebook and pencil next to your bed is a simple solution to a very frustrating problem. Dream journals don't

44

have to be as neat and tidy as a daily journal, since odds are you won't be fully functioning at 3 a.m. when you get that story idea. Bulleting, shorthand, and even sketches are perfect for a dream journal. As long as you can decipher it the next day.

The third type of journal I'd like to discuss—the kind I ask my students to keep, is called a *sondering* journal. Sonder, a word invented by John Koenig from *The Dictionary of Obscure Sorrows*, means "the realization that each random passerby is living a life as vivid and complex as your own—populated with their own ambitions, friends, routines, worries and inherited craziness—an epic story that continues invisibly around you like an anthill sprawling deep underground, with elaborate passageways to thousands of other lives that you'll never know existed, in which you might appear only once, as an extra sipping coffee in the background, as a blur of traffic passing on the highway, as a lighted window at dusk." Basically, you keep a journal featuring interesting characters you glimpse in real life and try to fill in the blanks as to who they are, what they do, what their aspirations are, etc. Like a diary entry for another person. This method has been overwhelmingly successful for students in generating vibrant, well-developed characters and images for writing assignments.

Planning: Chaos vs. Structure

While completing my MFA at Wilkes University in Wilkes-Barre, Pennsylvania, I had the pleasure of working with two faculty mentors who also happened to be married to each other. Both had published multiple acclaimed novels as well as found great success in academic writing, yet one was a strict, organized former Navy officer, while the other was a laid-back free spirit. Knowing my personal preference for minimal planning, I chose to work with the latter. My decision would not have served others well, as they need structure and timetables to thrive.

While I do believe planning is absolutely necessary in some form, others think it is the most important step of the process. Planning-heavy writers attribute a weeks-long (sometimes months or even years) process of plotting, outlining, character developing, and storyboarding to their publishing success. Taking time to deliberately plan your project can be of great benefit both to its completion and your own mental wellbeing. How much planning, or pre-writing, will you require?

Organize Your Thoughts
Through free writing, journaling, and planned writing, you should start to compile a significant amount of material to work with. Now to organize all of it. This is one area where chaos and clutter simply will not do. Because the desired end result of the invention process is to develop a manuscript of some sort, organization of materials is a must.

Organization is important for two main reasons: everything is easily accessible for use in the final stages of your project and the morale boost in seeing all of your work in one place. Keep your documents stored in a safe place with multiple copies or files in case a catastrophic loss claims one copy of the manuscript. Also, once the project is complete, keep all of your supplemental notes and documents for the revision process in folders, binders, or cabinets. There is no waste in the writing process. Be careful what you throw away.

Be Social—Join a Writers' Group
Writers, for the majority of their writing time, will be alone. Writing is innately a solitary activity. After days or

even weeks working on a project alone in one's writing space, social interaction is needed. The benefits of joining a group of likeminded individuals are tremendous.

First, you will need an open audience for your work. Writing groups are populated by people in the same situation you will find yourself. They also want a sounding board for what they have produced. Being willing to share your work and listen to others will benefit your morale in the long run. Who knows, you may build some strong relationships along the way.

Writers need reassurance that what they are working on has value. Having someone (preferably a person you are very comfortable with) read your manuscript when it is finished allows for feedback and notes to work from. It is best to share small sections you are feeling unconfident about while your project is a work in progress, but keep the big reveal for when it is complete. If you talk about your work too much and too often, you may lose the drive to actually put it down on paper. The theory is that once the story is out of you, why bother writing it?

Take Time For Yourself
Don't burn yourself out. Writing is often a monumental undertaking, so make sure you give yourself breaks from the work in order to boost your morale and keep your sanity. When you feel like you can't go on writing, take a few minutes to gather your thoughts, energize, and refocus. Trying to push through the fatigue will only lead to wasted time and discouragement. Take a walk around the neighborhood to clear your head.

During the actual physical writing process, my colleagues and I subscribe to the Pomodoro Technique® developed by Francesco Cirillo. This method uses twenty-five-minute timed intervals to produce followed by a short break to maximize performance. The process is broken down into five steps:

1. Choose your task and how many "pomodori" you will do
2. Set a timer for twenty-five minutes for each work "pom"
3. Work on the task until the timer goes off
4. Take a five-minute break to walk around, check messages, etc.
5. Take a thirty-minute break after completing four "poms" to stave off monotony

Utilizing this method has proven time and time again to be effective in time management and productivity in all forms of writing and research projects.

Just like with any job, you need time to yourself to decompress after the work is done. Stephen King suggests stepping away from a finished project for a "cooling off" period of anywhere from three weeks to three months. You can go back to it with fresh eyes in order to better understand what revisions are needed. When you have finished a draft of a manuscript, feel free to reward yourself with some time away from writing to avoid burn out. Everything will still be there when you get back.

Stay Positive
Writing is a lifestyle you have to commit yourself to, and over the years you will occasionally fail. It's as simple as that. We all do. Even putting in the time, effort, and strategies laid out in this chapter, you may come up short. Do not let failure stop you from writing. Too often, that is the case amongst emerging writers. Thomas Edison didn't

invent the light bulb in one or two tries. It took him over two thousand attempts to get it right. With that kind of perseverance, you can accomplish anything. Sure, writing can be tedious at times and you may feel yourself getting tired, but if you remember to keep the process enjoyable and to put your physical and mental health first, you will succeed.

Chapter Five

Revising Your Writing: Strategies for Improving
Your Work Draft by Draft

MARY ANN CAIN

You wrote something. Maybe it's inspired; maybe it's a
prompt from class; maybe you wrote just to write. Now
what?

You may already be thinking of writing as a process. As
other chapters in this collection indicate, there are many
dimensions to this process. But calling it a process is
different than nailing down a formula or identifying steps
in a "how-to" guide. Instead, process is a way of describing
an experience that all writers engage in but that, at the
same time, varies greatly from individual to individual.
Naming and investigating certain parts of an experience
that all writers share in some way can be helpful, especially
to developing writers. Revision is one of those parts.

Rather than look at revision as just something a writer
elects to do or not do, it is more helpful to start with the
assumption that all writers revise in some way, whether
they are aware that they are doing it or not. It might also
help to consider that revision, like process itself, is not,
strictly speaking, a linear experience. When we compose,
it's not that we go from A to B to C. Instead, a great deal
of recursivity—going back and forth—occurs, even as we
(eventually) move towards completion.

But first, it's important to come to a shared understanding
of terms. What is revision? More to the point, what do

I mean by this term? Nancy Sommers, in a comparative study in 1980, discovered a significant difference between what experienced adult writers meant and did by way of revision versus student writers. What she discovered, and what I've found to be largely true over decades of teaching writing, is that for many students, revision equals editing and proofreading: you write your draft, then go through and clean up "mistakes," sometimes on the global level ("Am I clear enough?" "Does this order make sense?" "Am I focused enough or just rambling or padding?" "Does the work 'flow'?") but more often on a sentence level ("Is this spelling correct?" "Is that the right word?" "Did I punctuate correctly?" "Is my grammar in general correct?" "Is the phrasing smooth?"). The purpose of such revision, then, is to "clean up" what's already been expressed, as if the overall thought is understood and simply in need of a tune-up.

As Cy Knoblauch and Lil Brannon note in their classic book on writing instruction, *Rhetorical Traditions and the Teaching of Writing*, most writing assigned for college students does not even invite revision beyond a first draft. Thus, it is no surprise that many students understand revision mainly as the final "clean-up" before turning in their writing for a grade. In contrast, what I consider revision is more in line with what Sommers found that experienced writers actually do. Revision is about going back and "re-visioning" (i.e. re-seeing) one's initial expressions, thoughts, and ideas through a different perspective. Revision is about extending the discovery process that begins when, as poet Diane Glancy describes, words rub together like "firesticks." It's about how to change perspective on this process and, in turn, the available choices along the way. It's also about changing direction—from focusing on meanings, thoughts, and ideas, and putting those into words, to focusing on the words, images, forms, genres, rhythms, patterns, figures of speech, etc. as they give rise to meaning, and vice versa.

When we think about what we intend to write, that thinking, as researchers have shown, actually encompasses many different operations in our bodies, including our brains. We "think" not only in words, but in images—sounds, colors, scents, textures, rhythms, tastes, and so forth. We are creatures of association—one thought, one image, one word, one story, makes us think of another. For autistic or other people with cognitive differences such as renowned animal scientist and autistic advocate Temple Grandin, however, "thinking" is not so much in words as in what she calls "pictures" (Grandin 1996). Yet this sort of thinking, which everyone does to a greater or lesser extent, involves revision, as one "picture" gives rise to another, until those "pictures" are committed to the page. From this perspective, you can see that revision begins the moment you start "picturing" what you might write.

However, we often perceive that transition—from thoughts to words to written words—as proceeding in only one direction: forward. We don't think about how the thought-pictures are being revised every time we reconsider how to capture them in words. Every time we look, they change. Instead, what can often happen is that we see ourselves as having great ideas for which we can't quite find the right words.

A useful aphorism to help disrupt this too-limited understanding of revision goes like this: "If we change the way we look at things, the things we look at change." Revision, then, is about, first, paying attention to how we are already always revising our thought-pictures, ideas, feelings, words, and second, how we can make more conscious use of this process towards greater creative and critical powers with language.

Unfortunately, some of the lore around writing—the collective, commonsensical stories that get passed on over time—posits that *not* knowing is what the creative process requires. There's a grain of truth to that. Similarly, the old saying that "too many cooks spoil the broth" is another bit of lore. But as with any creative work, it's more a question of how, when, and why, rather than seeing the choice simply as either accepting or rejecting critical responses. To take it to yet another level, part of revision is how to reframe your choices beyond simple binaries—my draft is either good or bad; I either keep going with this draft or I scrap it altogether. There are other choices: these become apparent when you start to pay attention to what is already happening as you compose.

Creative Destruction: Taking Risks in Learning How to Pay Attention

In *You Must Revise Your Life* poet William Stafford describes how one way to pay better attention is to reframe the binary way of looking at writing that we all do, namely to praise or blame what's been written. And even though we may not admit it, we may often feel that praise or blame extending to ourselves as writers. But to reframe our habitual ways of looking at drafts and at writers requires some creative disruptions. In this regard, creativity is intimately linked with destruction. Another way of putting it is to make the strange familiar and the familiar strange. Again, it goes back to perception, i.e. how we "look" at the word and the world. We need to shake things up, "change the way we look at things." This requires taking some risks.

In a classroom situation, when grades are at stake, when time is at a premium, when you don't have the (perceived) luxury of waiting for the muse to strike, of letting an idea percolate, of putting something away for future reference, taking risks can seem not only frightening but counterproductive. It goes against what we expect students to do, namely be efficient, productive, and forward-moving. However, creativity in general, and revision in particular, is a lot messier; it can seem inefficient, unproductive, and stagnant. But once you start to change the way you see this part of the process, what you see, and in turn, the choices available to you for how to proceed, can change, too.

In the exercises that follow, one big change in how you see is this: in the process of revising existing drafts, those revisions are not necessarily going to be better or worse. It's more useful, I think, to simply consider that they will be *different*. For some writers, moving away from the original thought-pictures behind a draft can be very intimidating. To try out other directions may lead to confusion. And if you are already confused with the existing draft, more confusion is not necessarily welcome. To this end, it's helpful to save drafts in separate word processing files on your computer. Once you begin another draft, open it in a new file. This is not to say that confusion will necessarily disappear. But it is to say that you can lessen that particular confusion by referring back to the original first draft. It is also to point out that confusion is part of the creative process in general, and revision in particular. It is a necessary risk.

To further reframe the revision process, it can help to understand how to revise our commonsensical understandings of not only revision in writing, but also in life. In *Getting Restless: Rethinking Revision in Writing Instruction*, Nancy Welch contrasts what most writing teachers and students assume about how writers learn with a less familiar but (I'd argue) more helpful way of looking at that process. Drawing upon psychoanalytical theory, Welch claims that our educational system, and by extension, American/Western culture, tends to assume that we learn through "identification and imitation." Instead, she challenges that assumption in favor of "facilitat[ing] the recognition and revision of what we're identifying with, who we are imitating—and what's being denied, suppressed, or perpetuated in the process" (Welch, *Getting Restless,* p. 56). So instead of looking at revision as a way to identify with what Knoblauch and Brannon call a teacher-identified Ideal Text (Knoblauch and Brannon, *Rhetorical Traditions*) and imitate existing models of that Ideal (i.e. what the teacher or other readers presumably "want" us to say and how to say it), we shift our perception to ask what in our texts, and in ourselves, is "being denied, suppressed, or perpetuated in the process" (by this Ideal Text).

One important implication of this reframing, from identification and imitation, to critical questioning and disruption of that process, is how we regard error. When we are perceiving a draft through the frame of "right or wrong," "good or bad," it's in part because we assume there is an Ideal that we should be striving for, whether we are conscious of such an Ideal or not. Knoblauch and Brannon

55

note how teacher responses to student writing perpetuate a sense of an Ideal Text among student writers: "A student's task is to match the Ideal Text in the teacher's imagination which is insinuated through the teacher's commentary, not to pursue personal intentions according to the writer's own developing sense of what he or she wishes to say" (*Rhetorical Traditions*, p. 120). Many, if not most, of the comments we may receive from teachers or other readers are directed towards steering us towards some Ideal that conforms to a more familiar, conventional mode of expression and, in turn, a more familiar way of looking at a subject. Even without outside feedback, we have mostly internalized this process of identification and imitation so well that we see our drafts and ourselves through it. To further complicate this process, it's difficult to even see how and when we are doing this, let alone understand what Ideal Text we may be (unconsciously) aiming for. Welch extends this idea of reframing an Ideal Text by noting how necessary: "…the classroom's tense, charged, and sometimes even erotic and antagonistic attachments are…to revision." Instead of regarding revision as the more typical "clean-up" model, Welch posits revision as a way to shift what we mean and how we identify not only in a text but also in our lives (Welch, *Getting Restless,* p. 55). So instead of seeing writing and revision as mainly a process of fitting in, which includes excising "errors" that prevent that conformity, Welch suggests that we reframe those places where we don't fit in, where we make errors, as opportunities for "intervening in the meanings and identifications" of our texts and of our lives. We re-vision that Ideal Text as a place to critically examine, take apart, and change for the sake of including those parts that at first don't seem to conform because they are too "strange." This is what being creative entails: working with and against what is the expected, Ideal, conventional, familiar, for the sake of fuller expression and a greater truth: making the strange familiar.

Exercises to Get You to Another, Different Draft
Now that I've mapped out what revision is and how it matters, here is where we can get into the practical aspects of how to engage in revision in more conscious, deliberate ways. Getting helpful comments from teachers, fellow students, and other writers and readers is useful but not absolutely necessary. You can begin revising on your own through the exercises that follow. This book's bibliography can also direct you to the sources I've referenced that might also provide more in-depth approaches to revision.

CHANGING UP THE PARTS
This exercise invites you to write a completely different draft that may be quite different not only in form and content but also (and perhaps especially) meaning. Here are some examples of what you might try.

Change the Main Character or Persona of the Piece
That's right: you can start again with an entirely different set of eyes through which to see the same experiences. All narratives, whether in a short story, poem, play, essay, or other genre, locate us in a particular way of looking, based on an imagined narrator/speaker. Even when we are writing "true" stories, as in creative nonfiction, or even academic or professional work, we still create a narrator who we may or may not identity with as ourselves. Starting again will no doubt lead to an entirely different piece. And

that's good, because revision is best when we have more than one version for the sake of comparison.

A variation on this would be to change point of view. So, for instance, instead of using first person "I" or "we," you would shift to third person "she" or "he," or vice versa. (You can also try second person, "you," although that's a bit more challenging.)

Another variation is to change up other elements. In fiction, you can change the object of a main character's motivation, both on a concrete level (Greg wants to ask out a woman he's obsessed with) and on an abstract level (Greg wants to overcome his shyness). You can also change the obstacles or challenges that the character or persona may be facing. In a poem, this might translate into shifting from focusing on one event or memory instead of another, one set of desires over another, even one beginning or ending over another.

Change the Order

Where you begin and end a piece has a great deal of power over how a draft develops. After you've completed a draft is a good time to consider changing the order. What happens in what sequence can be changed—for instance, from a chronological A to B to C, to B to C to A, and so forth. For many newer writers, the first impulse is to write in a "logical" order, which is often understood as chronological. But on an emotional and psychological level, chronological order misses a lot and can weigh down a piece because it commits you to include all sorts of nonessential actions and descriptions just to make the necessary transitions. So in changing the order of what happens, you free yourself to tap into more emotionally and psychologically driven associations and connections between the parts.

Let's say, for instance, that your first-draft poem begins with the color blue and a description of a lake. Let's say, too, that it ends with a walk through a vacant lot in the middle of a run-down city neighborhood. You might flip the beginning and the ending. You might even start in the middle. I've often found with narratives, for instance, that starting *in media res* (literally, "in the middle of the action") can make for a more focused, dramatically intensified beginning. Or even starting a few paragraphs in from the first draft's opening can be eye-opening. Creating a story "frame" in which the story begins and ends in present time, while the middle and main action of the story takes place in the past, can also help. Changing the order of stanzas and sections in a poem is similarly useful. Such revisions can help us refocus away from the expected, conventional way of looking and into something more unexpected, perhaps truer, but certainly different. Again, composing a second draft that provides a clear contrast to the first can be helpful in framing choices for how to continue that we might not otherwise have discovered.

Changing Form and Style

A great resource for all kinds of revision strategies comes from Wendy Bishop's collection, *Elements of Alternate Style: Essays on Writing and Revision*. Bishop, a composition scholar, poet, and teacher, had rediscovered a teacher-writer-scholar named Winston Weathers, who coined the term "grammar B" to describe ways of learning written conventions by way of breaking those conventions. In a chapter from Bishop's book by Elsie Rogers, entitled

"Stretch a Little and Get Limber: Warming up to (and With) Grammar B," Rogers takes readers through a series of revision exercises that focus on more local, immediate choices of style and form. While her exercises start with first drafts, these can easily be adapted to rewriting existing drafts. So, for instance, you might take a stanza or paragraph or section of dialogue or description and rewrite it using only one-syllable words. Compare and contrast what the effect of both drafts are: how were your choices affected given this new constraint? Rogers then opens the constraints a bit and allows no more than half the words to include two syllables, and for a sentence to be several words longer than the sentence that precedes it.

As Rogers explains, opening up form and style concurrently offers fresh choices in the meaning and focus of a piece. She sees such exercises as the necessary practice of writers, similar to musicians and athletes who do warm-up exercises prior to a more involved practice or performance. But beyond just warm ups, these approaches can be adapted for revision.

Adding Contrasting Emotions

This exercise comes from Nancy Welch, who in a workshop she led with my students, directed them to select a passage from their work and identify an emotion that colors that section. Then she had students rewrite that passage using a contrasting emotion. Note that she does not substitute one emotion for another but rather invites you to build complexity of feeling. Unlike our logical minds, the emotional part of our imaginations contain many contrasts and even contradictions; it's what makes us human. Conventional forms and meanings can direct us away from such contradictions as not "fitting" what is commonsensical. But it's those slips and breaks that this exercise in particular calls forth for a fresh perspective. It's what Welch calls "getting restless," looking at contrasts and contradictions as not something to cut out but as something creative to help us reframe how we look.

ADD ANOTHER, CONTRASTING VOICE OR CHARACTER

This can be accomplished in any number of ways. In my fiction classes, sometimes I direct students to add a new secondary character who can bring a fresh set of eyes to the story's action and outcomes. In a poem, it might be a second persona or simply stanzas or lines with a counterpoint tone, rhythm, pace, style, and so forth. The contrasting voices can be integrated into the original draft line by line, sentence by sentence, and/or stand alone in separate, alternating sections. The important part is to develop a voice that provides some sense of contrast—it may be harmonious or dissonant, but either way, you must include enough so that the additions seem part of the work rather than an anomaly.

RETHINKING ERROR: HOW TO DEAL WITH "MISTAKES"

Sometimes, when reading a draft, I'll notice words or phrases that, for whatever reason, stick out from the rest of the piece. It might be that the diction is more casual or formal; it may be a rhythm change; it may be a metaphor or other figure of speech that stands out from any others. Clichéd expressions sometimes fit this description, but also simply bits that sound really strong or weak compared to the rest.

The first impulse writers often have is to cut what doesn't fit. Cut out the clichés (they are bad, after all!), smooth out the tone, make the diction more consistent, and so forth. But this way of thinking limits revision to the one-directional "clean-up" task mentioned earlier. Instead, we can regard these "mistakes" as an opportunity to re-vision the focus and direction of a piece.

So, for instance, you might notice the word "red" is used ten times in three pages of prose or in a poem. Your first thought might be: I'm being redundant; get out the thesaurus. But then perhaps the problem isn't that you use that word too much; it may be that you need to do more repetition in general as part of the style and tone of the piece. Maybe the repetition can conjure a useful obsessive quality that plays into emotional resonance. Maybe not just colors but images can be repeated, with notable variations, as in a musical score. The meaning will likely follow.

Clichés, on the other hand, are rarely something to leave as is. But simply cutting them out is to miss creative opportunities. I've heard writers call them "place holders" for something else, something different and less conventional or familiar. Giving a cliché a new twist is a fun way of using language to lead towards meaning and re-vision. An expression such as "from cradle to grave" can be revised as "from cradle to boat launch" or "from starlight to grave." Of course, the difficult part is seeing clichés. Reading out loud can help.

READ YOUR WORK OUT LOUD
It surprises me how few writers, whether seasoned or newer, ever read their work out loud. When writers come to give readings at our university, more than a few wield a pen or pencil and make notes on their manuscripts as they read to an audience. (Personally, I make mental notes.)

Why, you might ask? Because hearing our words gives us a different experience than simply seeing them on the page. You embody the sounds, rhythms, tones, paces, and pauses or stops. There is a visceral, vibratory sense of the language as material, real, active. In a workshop I took with author Toni Morrison years ago, she asked us to read drafts out loud. We did not get to read anything from the page. Author Betty Edwards describes how different sides of the brain perform different sorts of operations, and right-sidedness corresponds with more global, wholistic "pictures," as opposed to the left-sided, more analytical aspects of thought. Reading out loud can give an immediate sense of where the words sag or slow down, or conversely, rush past. We can also more readily sense depth of feeling, even if we don't necessarily understand the logical dimensions of the writing. While poetry may seem to draw more upon the global, sensed experience of language, all forms rely upon both sound and sense.

Read your drafts out loud to yourself. Better yet, get someone to listen, just listen, as you read. I find that the simple act of having someone listen sharpens my own felt sense of a draft.

"You Must Revise Your Life"

In conclusion, I circle back to poet William Stafford's words regarding a life's work of writing and writing workshops. In embracing revision, you are embracing a different, albeit more subtle, approach to life.

[I]f you are a student, you may find in yourself a continuing way of life that is enriched by the practice of art. What you might have identified as your goal—publication, fame, praise— you may discover to be incidental to satisfactions that come

63

with working out by means of the materials of art the values and needs of your central being[...] You find that a workshop is not just a test; it is a concentrated encounter with experiences that relate to what you have chosen to do. (Stafford, *You Must Revise Your Life*, p. 103)

Chapter Six

Presenting Your Writing: How to Give a Reading of Your Work

GARRY CRAIG POWELL

I'm in grad school, at a public reading at the University of Arizona. The hall is packed, the audience eager: the poet onstage, an aging, tallish man in an elegant cream calico suit, is one of the most famous in the country. He is going to read from a book-length poem about a tropical island. The moment he begins, he puts on a different voice, a "poet's voice"—obviously intended to be dramatic, it rises and falls, but in unnatural places. You can tell where the end of every line is because his pitch sharpens as if someone muscular were crushing his knuckles painfully. Never once does he pause or look at the audience. The words are beautiful enough, euphonious, and the imagery striking—but he reads them as if he were reading a language he did not know well. The meaning is lost in the random sing-song fluctuations, and although he is consciously avoiding the monotone, his affected intonation does become monotonous. My ten-year-old son slides off his chair as if his spine will no longer support him, and despite my quiet attempts to pull him back up, remains on the floor. He begins crawling under the seats. To him this is far more entertaining than listening to the distinguished poet. At first I am embarrassed: he is ten, not two! Then, looking at the faces of the audience members, which are glazed and polite, like those of a church congregation, I realize that

I can't blame him. I too would rather crawl beneath the forest of legs than feign interest in this pointless blather. Naturally, at the end of the reading, which seems to go on for several hours, there is a thunderstorm of clapping—even literary people generally applaud the reputation rather than the work—but afterwards, when I find two of my MFA classmates, they agree with me: the man may be able to write, but he can't read.

I could regale you with many such stories, but there is no need: you too have been at the reading where the poet murmured in a voice so timid that you caught only half of what she said, where the novelist read so expressionlessly that she might well have been reading her bills, and the short-story writer bored you for ten minutes explaining how he thought of the story, apologizing for its awfulness, and then read it from his phone, so fast you thought he might be on speed, losing his place, apologizing again, laughing nervously, and finally scurrying off stage as if he had just committed some shameful act.

And perhaps he had: because it is, if not a crime, at any rate an offense of sorts, to waste people's time at a public performance. If you accept an invitation to read your work in public, you are tacitly proclaiming two things to the audience: first, that you have valuable work to share with them, something moving, funny, thought-provoking, perhaps disturbing, beautiful, haunting—something that will enlarge the listener's vision of the world or some aspect of it. Second, you are saying that you are a writer, not a bumbling amateur—otherwise, why would anyone want to listen to you? If you genuinely think of yourself as a bumbling amateur, you should either stay at home or practice until you sound like a professional.

Here's the bad news: most people are terrible readers when they give their first performances. And here's the good news: you can and will get better. It's not simply a matter of innate talent, although, as with writing itself, that plays a part. But your performance can improve immeasurably if you learn a few simple techniques. The purpose of this essay is not so much to teach you what those techniques are, as to remind you, because in fact you already know them, intuitively.

A good way to begin is to listen to masters of the public performance of literature, like Dylan Thomas—his readings of his hilarious stories are even better than those of his poetry—or Richard Burton, reading Thomas's *A Child's Christmas in Wales* or his own tale *A Christmas Story*. Writers from the British Isles have the advantage of a naturally melodious dialect, and this is especially true of the Welsh, but even if you are from North America, and have a naturally flatter, more monotonous prosody, you can learn to modulate your voice, as actors do. The NPR show *Selected Shorts*, which broadcasts short fiction every Wednesday night, has professional actors reading, almost all of them American, and most of the deliveries are excellent, if occasionally melodramatic.

The trick is to read the words as if you mean them. That means reading them slowly enough to think about them, and feel them as you say them. If you do this, you will emphasize the important words, stress the right syllables; your voice will rise with indignation, fall at the end of a period, pause now and then, taut and tense, with wonder or tenderness. If you are reading right, you are seeing the images as you speak, and hearing and smelling and tasting and touching them: you are spinning a world.

Singers know that if they are not moved by their songs, neither will their audiences be. It is the same with writers, as Robert Frost knew. Feel it. It doesn't matter if you are nervous. As Detroit poet Jamaal May says in his blog post on *Poets & Writers*, you can use that energy and transform it. Your body gives you adrenaline for a purpose: anthropologists call it the three-F response: flight, fight, and, to put it euphemistically, 'fornicate'. You want to do one or both of the last two: make love with the audience or enter into combat with them. Frighten them, disturb them, overpower them; cajole, caress, convince, flirt. But don't run. Incidentally, May has more good advice. He counsels you to read in your own voice. Practice as if you're speaking your lines or your prose to a friend. You want to sound natural.

The most common weaknesses of inexperienced readers is that they read too fast and with too little expression. Both are the result of the writer facing the task as a chore. Some writers actually claim that they do not wish to give a performance; they do not want to be seen as melodramatic. The irony of this position, as May points out, is that a wooden reading actually seems even more false than an overly dramatic one, because no one speaks in a flat monotone, at any rate when discussing anything vital, exciting or moving. So slow down; engage the audience. Remember that what you are doing, whether you like it or not, *is* a performance. Stop now and then and look at the audience. Not at the audience as a faceless crowd, either, but at individuals. Notice the expressions on their faces. You will see and feel if your words are having the effect you intended. This is immensely valuable for you as a writer—indeed, it may be the most accurate response you can get to your published work. Audiences will often fake their applause out of politeness, but they do not fake their responses to the words as they hear them. Understand that in a public reading, the meaning is not merely what is on the page, what you have written—it is being negotiated, moment by moment, with a group of human beings. Again I return to the analogy with music. What happens in the room, sometimes, if you are lucky, is that the work transcends itself: it has not only the meaning you intended to give it, but all the multifarious meanings your listeners find in it, all their personal memories and associations that are conjured up, all their identifications, so it is as if a new story or poem were being created. You find people laughing in places you did not expect, or weeping in what you thought was a comic story. Remember that the origin of poetry is in music, as our word "lyrical" attests, and the words "enchantment," "incantation" and "chant" are etymologically very close. Song and spell are the same. All good literature, whether verse or prose, is musical, melodious, rhythmical. Hear your poem as a song, your story as a sonata, your novel or memoir as a symphony or opera.

This is what Mark Spitzer means in his hilarious video, "Pointers for Performance of Poetry and Prose", when he commands you to "own it." He says that every word should "burn, burn, burn." Of course it should! If it is lukewarm, why serve it up? Spitzer also advises readers to practice—pause at the end of stanzas and paragraphs, check pronunciation of difficult words, decide what to emphasize—and ham it up. Don't just read, he says. Use hand gestures, theatrical inflections, build to a crescendo. I agree—as long as it comes naturally to you. Don't force yourself, or you will come across as artificial, inauthentic. But even if you are shy by nature, you can learn to make eye contact with your audience, speak with natural intonation, and give your listeners time to digest what you are reading.

I do not wish to make a list of things not to do at a reading, because positive instructions have more effect upon us than negative ones. (It is invariably more productive to tell someone to remember something than to tell them not to forget it.) Nevertheless, writer and blogger Dylan Kinnett has a useful list, which consists mainly of advice on how to avoid looking and sounding like a neophyte—what I have called the bumbling amateur. Here are some of his points: don't tell the audience that you just wrote this. It's impolite because it suggests that you either had nothing significant written beforehand, or dashed off something, anything, as a chore. Don't diss your own work, for if you don't like it, how can you expect anyone else to? Nor should you mention anyone else who likes it, especially your mother! Don't overexplain; let the work speak for itself. (No spoilers!) And don't riffle through papers: be ready. To this last, I might add: print your work in large type. Do not read from your phone. It looks unprofessional, and you will either find yourself struggling to read type in a small font, or else, if you have made the font large, you will have so little text in front of your eyes that you will lose the meaning.

In his essay "How to Deliver a Poetry Reading", Adam Robinson declares that the necessary elements for a great poetry reading are great poetry and great presence. Of course you could substitute "fiction" or "nonfiction" for "poetry" as well. No matter how well you read, if the content isn't enthralling, it will probably fall flat.

However, it's also true, and less understood, that even if your content is superb, if you don't read it well, it will still fall flat. Perhaps the greatest reader I know is Naomi Shihab Nye. Although it is often given as an axiom that one cannot read for long without boring an audience—some say the maximum is twenty minutes, some half an hour; the longest I have ever heard given as the upper limit is forty minutes—I have twice heard Naomi read, each time for well over two hours, and on one of those occasions for almost three hours (although she sang a couple of songs on that occasion, of her own composition, accompanying herself on a guitar.) And the audience was enthralled. No one, I think, left the auditorium. On each occasion, I took careful note of the expressions of the audience, to see if they had been as transported as I had by her poetry and stories. And their faces fairly shone with excitement; they glowed with happiness; they looked more alive, grander and more beautiful. Person after person came up to her afterwards and thanked her, telling her how much that reading had meant to her, how deeply they had been moved. The intensity of the emotion was overwhelming. It is not an exaggeration to say that it was a spiritual experience, an uplifting one that enriched the lives of the listeners. So how does Naomi do it?

For a start, although she reads for a long time—a very long time indeed—she never reads one piece for more than five or ten minutes. And she varies her material a lot, switching genres, switching mood—she will go from poem to personal narrative, from funny to heartbreaking, from very brief to longer. She tells short, pithy stories between the stories, not tedious tales of the genesis of her work; she adds context. She talks as if conversing with a friend.

71

She has a deep, rather husky, loud voice, which is a little startling, coming from her petite frame. She sounds as if she is enjoying herself immensely, because she is. She is ravished by language, and you can tell it from the way she enunciates every word clearly, lingering lovingly on the sweet ones and the soft ones, as well as the harsh and painful ones. As a writer, she is always aware of the spiritual dimension of her work—I realize I am discussing how to give a good reading, not appreciating a particular writer, but I believe there is a good deal of overlap here—and because every word she writes has the purpose of understanding others better, of putting us in unfamiliar shoes and thus helping us become more tolerant and kinder, her work transforms the world, and although you feel the world becoming better as you read it, you feel it even more as you listen to her. She is illuminated by her words. I once heard Michael Chabon speak for an hour about how his goal was to entertain. Good for him: he does. But Naomi Shihab Nye has a higher purpose: it is communion. More, it is transubstantiation. Just as the Catholic believes that the wine and wafer become the blood and flesh of Christ, words can become the world—and not merely the workaday world, but a transfigured world, a better world, the world made spirit. You do not have to believe in any religion to understand this.

Communion, transformation, transubstantiation: is this affected, pretentious nonsense? I hope not! If the goal of art is not to change us and change the world, make us see and feel more clearly and more deeply, then I have no idea what it is. And I think that if you write and read well, savoring your words, speaking them as if they were sacred—because they should be—then you are more than a scribbler, more than some singer in a cocktail lounge performing covers of sentimental hits: you are troubadour, priest, shaman. You are a myth-maker. You are engaged in a ritual that literally re-creates the universe. There is no higher calling. Remember that when you read.

Chapter Seven

The Critical and Reflective Study: How to Write It and Why

DIANNE DONNELLY

> The exegesis [the critical and reflective study] is a fascinating hybrid creature with a claw firmly embedded in two bodies: the arts and academia.
>
> (Jeri Kroll 2004, p. 2)

Suspending Your Disbelief: An Overview

Do you know how when you're watching a movie and you suspend your disbelief and accept the dystopian future in *The Hunger Games*; or buy into the fact that Luke Skywalker's limited Jedi training with Yoda in *The Empire Strikes Back* is somehow enough to keep him on par in a saber duel with his father Darth Vader; or you may even accept, for that matter, the existence of time travel, extraterrestrial life, zombies, wolverines, transformers, and superheroes.

Your willing suspension of disbelief affords you the opportunity to put aside your skepticism for the sake of a good story and to become drawn into and accept a consensual reality. In a sense, suspending your disbelief is what I want you to do here as you read this chapter on writing critical and reflective studies because my goal is to convince you that a parallel universe coexists in creative writing. Let's call it a multiverse, one which integrates the critical and creative by framing your creative work with a critical study that not only advances your creative work, but also deepens your understanding about the dynamic processes of your writing, the choices you make and the consequences of these choices, the way you synthesize new knowledge and rework this new understanding into your own writing practices, and the way your study of writing through writing can lead to new insights, conclusions, and newly acquired knowledge.

Suspending your disbelief also means shifting your focus away from the preconceived notion that your success in a creative writing course/program is measured solely on the end result of your creative work: your completed short story collection or portfolio of poems, dramatic plays, novellas, or novels. Rather, I suggest there is value in merging and aligning the critical and reflective components with the creative components and exploring the discoveries that are associated with your creative processes, all of those writerly creative acts and actions you perform that lead to the knowledge that is embedded in your individual experiences and internalized and practiced through your immersion in these writing activities. Such processes reflect the nature of creative writing as a practice-led research discipline—an area of study that is focused on the nature of practice and the ways in which this practice leads to new understanding and knowledge. It is the *critical and reflective study* of this recursive and fluid activity that considers creative writers' personal drive to discover and develop knowledge that can assist with their creative projects that this chapter addresses.

In a Nutshell, What Is the Critical and Reflective Study?
The critical and reflective study is a *sustained* account of your creative work. Think of it as an ongoing, dynamic

engagement of your creative processes; a place for discussion, a site of contextualization and interrogation, and a method by which you can better understand your writing journey, not as a passive responder might at the completion of her work (as an afterthought or "tag-on" to what's already a finished product), but as an active, present writer who is engaged in process and learning throughout the *whole* creation of her work—as a means "to study in, through, and about the art form" (Krauth, 2002). I'll get into more specifics in terms of what to record in your critical and reflective study and what physical space your study might take and how you might organize your study. But for now, I want to encourage you to be open to a dynamic activity that is written during the acts and actions of your creative work and that serves as "a framing device positioned between the world created in the fiction (or play or poem) and the world the reader inhabits" (Krauth 2002). As such, the critical and reflective study provides opportunities for writers to "speak twice about the literary nerves of their work, about the creative mechanisms driving it, and about the personal and cultural orientations that inform and frame and guide it" (Krauth 2002). Similarly, Jeri Kroll describes this study as a means of "allowing the audience to listen to the author speaking to herself before, during and after the act of creation" (2004, p. 7).

Because there is a symbiotic relationship of the critical and creative, you get to reflect on your learning process, your development, and your growth as a writer. You get to reflect on what you did and why you did it; what you changed or left out and why; the theories behind your approaches; your ideas and pre-existing personal experiences and cultural backgrounds; themes, research;

choices and consequences of these choices; considerations during revisions of iterations; characteristics of genre employed; influences in shaping your creative work; rationale for techniques and strategies embedded in your work; discoveries; and conclusions that inform your creative work as well as evidence of knowledge gained throughout the creative writing process.

Writing as Performance
We have no trouble thinking of such activities as singing, playing an instrument, painting, or dancing as *performance*—they all require specific "doing" actions. And I don't propose to know much about any of these activities except to know that steps like finding your vocal range; playing vibrato; detailing color, intensity, saturation, and texture; and designing motion, form, and space are practices of these performances. Think of *writing as a performance* as well—as an action—as an activity that is often made up of all that messy stuff—the dead ends, the starts and stops, the digressions, the twists and turns as well as the discoveries, surprises, the moments when the story takes shape or the poem emerges or the play unfolds—and when new realizations about our creative work and evolvement as a writer occur.

Knowledge Creation in Creative Writing
Taking this idea of writing as performance one step further is the understanding that the act of creative writing is associated with knowledge creation, not the kind that is associated with certainty as traditional models might claim—you know—the scientific method of testing a hypothesis through observation, measurement, and

experimentation. Rather, the knowledge in creative writing is in the discovery that takes you, as the writer, beyond the routines of writing, in the questions that arise and that are answered through your writing process. Barbara Guest, for example, talks about "an invisible architecture often supporting the surface of the poem, interrupting the progress of the poem," and she situates this architecture "in the period before the poem finds an exact form and vocabulary" (2002). In other words, "something else is happening" as you engage with the writing. Guest notes the "interruptions" that seem to occur...the poem begins to quiver, to hesitate, to become insubstantial...Yet the unstableness of the poem is important." Similarly, Barbara Bolt explains that the "new" (think new directions, new knowledge) emerges through writing processes as "a shudder of an idea, which is then realized in and through language" (2004). For Toni Morrison, it is the "What if?" that "squeezes an image forward." The writing that seeks the knowledge is represented in the creative work and contained as well in the critical and reflective study of the creative writing because the study *accounts* for the process, for the thoughts/actions/knowledge associated with writing the creative work. Such processes teach Morrison, for example, that she can't just "reach some little plateau and say that's it, this is the place. It is always a search" (Morrison, qtd. in Houston, 2009).

Defining Our Work/Process
Those "What if?" moments help us to better define our creative work—what's behind my decision to begin my story (or poem or play) as I did? Why create this setting? This timeframe? What if my story were told in first person?

How do my choices change the reading and meaning of my creative piece? Why does a flashback work here? A flashforward? What if instead of writing a summary of events, I created a dynamic scene? What's to be gained? What's to be lost? Why is this poetry scheme effective? Why choose this poetry form and pattern? Where do I add concrete, vivid details? In what way is my poem efficient and yet powerful? How does pacing affect my work? What does my protagonist desire, and what is getting in her way? What is the unstable ground situation (the crisis that exists prior to the story start)? How and where are my analogies and metaphors original and fresh? What creative works have influenced my creative development? How have my images stimulated the senses of my readers? Where have I led with concrete rather than abstract words/ideas? How have my word choices, dialogue, and/or narration affected my story? What experiences and/or context associated with social/political/environmental/economical/historical/cultural phenomena impact my work? Where have I subverted the ordinary so readers see an insider's view or perceive something in different and intriguing ways? Where is the conflict in my creative piece? How have I energized the dramatic dialogue of my play? What processes/conventions did I consider in the writing of a particular genre? What intentional crossing of genre conventions did I explore and why, and to what effect? If I blurred genres and/or experimented with digital technology and spatial configurations in my text, what techniques did I employ and why, and what are the effects of my efforts? What challenges did I face during the writing process, why did they surface, and what strategies did I use to overcome these challenges? How does research, the gathering of evidence that supports details in my story (or poem or play), unfold in my practice of writing? How have I added texture that gives my creative work credibility and the sense that anything like research has ever taken place?

You can see, in this list of process particulars, how the critical and reflective study becomes a communication tool between you and the "materials" that account for your ongoing journey as well as a platform for sharing processes with readers and instructors who may respond to your critical and reflective study as a portal to your creative work. As you assess your work from a process perspective, I would encourage you to look for patterns, to address methods of development, to reflect on revisions, to clarify concepts, and reveal perspectives. The critical and reflective study becomes a channel by which you can access all of the chaotic moments, catastrophes, rhythms, interruptions, quiverings, hesitations, unstableness, shudders, What If's?, searches, and discoveries, and it also becomes a conduit by which to make meaning of your practice, to think more metacognitively (i.e. to think about your thinking and make sense of what's been learned), and to generate newly acquired knowledge as a creative writer.

How Do I Write Critical and Reflective Studies?
There is no universal model for writing the critical and reflective study in concert with your creative work, but there are several foundational principles to follow and some suggestions to consider.

READ WIDELY
There is significant benefit to being informed, so read within and beyond your genre to explore any historical,

geographical, topical, cultural, linguistic, theoretical, and academic work that might broaden your perspective, expand your knowledge base, as well as add to your writing toolkit and clarify and substantiate your awareness and credibility of what you write.

Many practicing writers annotate the margins of the work they read so as to keep track of their reader responses—to jot down effective techniques, writers' choices and effects of choices, questions, links to their own writing, or points to further explore. All of these close readings or reading-as-a-writer approaches influence your writing in meaningful ways and connect you not only to your own model of writing, but to the models of other writers and critical thinkers and the ways in which these writers/thinkers contribute to the body of human knowledge.

FORMULATE SOME MECHANISM FOR DISPLAYING AN ACCOUNT OF YOUR WRITING PROCESS

Record your process in a physical space that allows you to revisit your writing process often. Such an archive might include a (1) hard-copy or computerized register of your writing process (a writing process journal), (2) digitalized documentation on, say, Google Docs or on a blog site, (3) hybridization of your creative and critical work in the form of footnotes and/or hyperlinks that integrate within the creative work and engage a target audience on multi-levels of intersection. You might even create a remediation that considers the textuality of the creative process in more interactive, digital ways.

A writing process and research journal allows you to account for all of your processes so that you can formulate, at any point in your creative work, your collective thoughts

81

and analysis. A few caveats before you get started. You want your journal to record meaningful data rather than superficial and anecdotal information that does *not* connect your knowledge creation with the act of writing. Don't think of this journal as a calendar of tasks completed or a "personal diary" in which you share your emotional relationship with your work. Your task is to demonstrate your process and your newly acquired knowledge and to offer evidence that demonstrates the connection between both creative and critical components.

If you delay recording your creative processes until the completion of the creative work, you will miss valuable opportunities to draw from the *evidence* of your sustained accounts of your process, and as a result, your analysis rests solely on your work as a final product rather than as a discovery of your acts and actions. When students don't show and consider their processes as they write, their critical reflections risk becoming superficial, at best, and not significantly a meaningful creative and academic exercise. They miss engaging with the moments associated with writing, the interstitial moments (the in-between writing moments), and all of the analytical learning processes of writing that help writers to develop their skills.

Today there are exciting multimodal technologies and programs that may also offer you opportunities to account for your work. In lieu of a hard copy or computerized copy of your critical and reflective study, you can organize your writing process account in a more digital way. You can create a website or a blog or engage with a digital software program that creates a living document that may include a range of representations and interpretations of your work in progress. For example, a website or blog might include hyperlinks to readings and research, embedded visual renderings and videos, and entries associated with reflections and processes. Topical links might also include historical and geographical markers that could assist with situating your piece in a cultural context. Rich data can speak to local and regional places and significances. Such a multimodal platform can provide a dimensional perspective that embraces new ways of using and communicating knowledge. The interplay between the creative work and the critical and reflective study is endless.

RECORD YOUR PROCESS BEFORE, DURING, AND AFTER YOUR CREATIVE WORK

Your creative and critical study is a place where you show your ideas, progress, problems, intentions, transitions, and newly acquired knowledge as well as where you document your research and the influences of your research.

You might (1) *preface your work* in this journal by considering your purpose, goals (what you hope to achieve), underlying assumptions, intentions, audience, writing and reading history along with research questions/ inquiries, influences of other artists, etc. As (2) an *ongoing interrogation of your process*, you should account for all of your writing process choices, considerations, and new insights that occur. The writing process chronicle is not meant to be an interruption of your creative work, but rather an impetus for propelling your writing forward and as a means for gaining new insight and knowledge. The more in-depth and detailed your recordings, the greater your perspective and analysis will be and the more insight you will have as to the new knowledge you have gained. As your writing process and research account will explore your creative processes at multiple intersecting points, you will have, at the completion of your creative work, a thorough record of your process and thinking, a compilation of your strengths and weaknesses, and an understanding of how your work developed over your continued process of writing. Through your research activity and annotations from your readings, iterations of your work, recordings of your processes and influences, notes from your instructor and workshop groups—all of the components mentioned in this chapter—you can then flip back on your writing processes and reflect on your knowledge gained throughout your writing processes and (3) *offer a substantive analysis of your writing processes that sits alongside your creative work* and that speaks to your development of new skills and new and/or varied ways of thinking as a result of working on your creative work. In organizing this final analysis you might consider in the *introduction*, a synopsis of your creative work, purpose/aims, audience, and aspects of your creative processes that you will discuss; the *analysis section* should detail your writing choices and considerations and provide an active accounting of your writing process and connections to learning paradigms; the *conclusion section* would offer a summary of what was discovered and achieved and what new practices may have opened up as a result of the writing processes.

Conclusion and Further Thoughts

While it may be a new concept for you to consider an analysis of your creative process that complements your creative work, and while there may be a tendency to see a critical and reflective study as less exciting and as holding less weight than the product of your creative work, performing this kind of analysis is such a critical part of understanding your creative process and your role as a developing writer. Because the critical and reflective study "is a reflection on those realizations that occur in our writing process and a recording of our active practices before, during, and after our creative work, we become open to what emerges in the interaction," with what Emmanuel Levinas calls "the materials of practice" (qtd. in Bolt), and through these material dealings, "we gain access to the world in an original and an ordinary way." (Levinas, qtd. in Bolt). There is value in revealing those aspects of your process which may not be readily apparent in your creative work; and as a dynamic process, the critical and reflective study informs and influences the progression and direction of your creative work. In the end, you have a dynamic complement of creative and critical components that speaks twice to your writing journey!

Chapter Eight

Grading Creative Writing: How It's Done and Why

JULIE PLATT

When you hear the words "grading" and "creative writing" in the same sentence, do you do a double-take? Do you feel like there might be a glitch in the Matrix? You can grade a set of math problems. You can grade a lab report. You can certainly grade a research paper (*Do you have a thesis statement? Did you use a minimum of eight sources? Did you write at least 2000 words?*). Creative writing, on the other hand, seems incompatible with grading. How can a teacher give a "C" or even a "D" to an honest and heartfelt poem, or to a short story with quirky and endearing characters, or to an essay that searches for the extraordinary in the ordinary?

It does seem very strange or even unfair to put a letter grade on something that seems to come from emotions or the imagination. But if you're reading this book, you know that creative writing requires much more than feeling something deep. It requires spending many hours closely studying the poems, stories, and essays we admire, and the hard work and skill of honing our own craft. It requires stoicism to solicit honest feedback from peers and mentors, and good judgment to evaluate and use that feedback in revising creative work. In short, you know that creative writing is real and rigorous. I and many others agree. Creative writing deserves to be held to the same high academic standards as other majors found in American colleges and universities, which means that creative writing courses and assignments cannot be given automatic "As". Grading and assessment have an important function in the higher educational system, and in that system, creative writing classes must be taken seriously.

Despite all this, grading creative writing can still be a murky concept. It helps to understand what grading actually is and why it's an important element in learning to *make* creative writing, and in learning to *be* a creative writer. In this chapter, I will first offer definitions of the terms *grading* and *assessment*, and describe the kinds of tools that are used as *formative* and *summative* assessments in creative writing. Next, I will discuss the kinds of creative writing courses one can find in colleges and universities in North America, highlighting what's typically assigned and graded in each kind of course. Finally, I'll conclude with some practical tips for how you can use your experiences with grading to grow into a stronger, more confident, and more self-aware creative writer.

Defining Terms
ASSESSMENT VS GRADING

Grading and assessment are two forms of *evaluation*, or the process by which one makes some kind of judgment. Everyone who has received even a little bit of formal education has heard the word *grading* and can give a reasonably accurate definition. However, the word *assessment* can be more elusive. While it's easy to use them interchangeably, these words do have very important differences in meaning, and those differences become more apparent when the words are used in particular contexts.

Let's start with assessment. According to education researchers K. Patricia Cross and Thomas A. Angelo (1988), assessment is the process of gathering data to learn about learning. In other words, assessment is a way of determining if a course, curriculum, or program of study is producing desired learning outcomes. In assessment, faculty often collaborate with each other—or even with students—in establishing these learning outcomes and creating the tools needed to test them. For example, a typical student learning outcome in a first-year writing class might say that "students should be able to write clear and arguable thesis statements." Instructors would explain this learning outcome to students, and present lessons and assignments for students to complete. If an instructor or team of instructors wanted to assess how well students were learning desired skills, they would likely develop a tool (like a rubric), choose a random sampling of student work, and evaluate the work anonymously. These instructors would then analyze the data produced from these evaluation sessions and discuss their connections to specific teaching practices. In response to this assessment, faculty and administrators would research and develop new teaching methods, assignments, and other course components to pilot, and then assess, in classrooms. This entire assessment process is collaborative, often applied on a large scale, and takes a great deal of time—months or years, in most cases.

On the other hand, grading has a different but related purpose. Grading is concerned with elements that are classroom based and have more to do with students' performance than with programmatic learning goals. Going back to the example of a first-year writing class, students might be graded on things such as class participation, timely and satisfactory completion of assignments and papers, or even preparedness and class attendance. Unlike assessment, grading is usually applied to the performance of individual students (or groups, if group work is assigned), so a first-year writing student might be graded on whether he or she was prepared for and participated in class discussions of assigned readings. The instructor, usually working alone, would compare student performance to grading criteria, and determine a way to represent the student's performance, usually with some kind of score or letter grade.

FORMATIVE VS SUMMATIVE

Another way to look at the differences between assessment and grading is to consider two specific types of evaluation: *formative* and *summative*. As a teacher myself, I see the relationship between these two as similar to the relationship between assessment and grading. Formative evaluation is concerned with monitoring student learning while it happens, and deciding what learning interventions need to happen. This is reflected in specific practices in which a teacher determines if students need, say, extra instructional class time to practice applying a concept, or a lesson presented in a different mode or style. Summative evaluation compares student work against some kind of established standard, in sum or in total. This is why summative evaluation usually happens at the ends of learning units or whole courses, when an instructor can make a judgment about the overall quality of student work. Formative evaluations are frequently described as "low stakes" because they have low, or even no, grade point value. Summative evaluations are described as "high stakes" because their grade point values are high and contribute significantly to determining the student's overall grade for the course. Most instructors use some combination of both formative and summative evaluation in their classrooms.

In creative writing programs, formative evaluations track learning while it is happening and while it can still be shaped. The ones I'll discuss here are the peer-led writing *workshop*, the individual *writer's notebook*, and self-evaluative (and instructor-guided) *reflection*. The most recognizable kind of formative evaluation in creative writing programs is the *workshop*. In workshop, first-draft student pieces and the discussion and feedback they receive are rarely assigned a measurable point value; this may be why workshops are not typically thought of as evaluative experiences. Yet a student offers a piece for critique, and other students and the instructor will discuss the piece and how it might be revised. The student's learning is evident in the way he or she is able to receive, understand, and evaluate criticism, and produce a stronger revised piece afterward. Therefore, the workshop functions as a kind of collaborative formative evaluation, with many voices shaping each student's growth as an artist. The rules of workshop might vary according to individual instructors' philosophies and student preferences. For example, some instructors prefer to use the so-called "Iowa method" (whose origins are outlined below) in which the student whose work is being critiqued is asked to refrain from speaking while the other students are discussing.

Another kind of formative evaluation is the *writer's notebook* or *journal*. The format of these varies by instructor and by program, but they can range from being simple logs of writing time, to diary entries exploring particular writing issues, to a place for a writer to collect and experiment with the ideas and sketches that make up a writing project. I was asked to keep one of these notebooks in an undergraduate poetry class. My professor periodically collected these and gave us credit for making regular entries, but he did not grade the content. Instead, he tracked our learning in a third formative way: *reflection.*

It's important for creative writers to practice reflection as a way of tracing their craft learning and their artistic vision, among other things. Reflection in creative writing happens when the writer looks back on an experience, event, or idea and analyzes it, considering its meaning in the context of that writer's growth. Experienced writers practice reflection frequently. Many times in creative writing programs, you will be expected to discuss these issues in ways that reflect critical understanding and artistic maturity. Instructors often ask students to write brief reflections on individual creative pieces, or about entire courses or semesters. Capstone projects such as program portfolios, theses, and dissertations almost always have a reflective component, such as those described in chapter 7; instructors usually offer students guidelines and examples for how to write these reflective pieces effectively.

As mentioned above, *summative* evaluation is concerned with the overall quality of work when compared to established criteria. Summative evaluations frequently provide the bulk of the formal grades expressed in point values, percentages, or letters. At the beginning of a course, the instructor should explain all assignments that receive summative evaluations and how those evaluations will construct the overall course grade. Instructors may also provide *rubrics* for these assignments. A rubric is a document that lists the criteria by which something will be evaluated. Below is an example rubric I developed for grading poems produced by a haiku exercise.

Haiku Exercise Grading Rubric			
Demonstrates Exceptional Proficiency (40 points)	Demonstrates Advanced Proficiency (30 points)	Demonstrates Basic Proficiency (20 points)	Needs Improvement (10 points)
Movement			
The poem features a skillfully crafted volta (poetic turn) which makes a fresh association and offers a profound sense of awareness and mindfulness.	The poem features a well-crafted volta which makes a unique association and offers a strong sense of awareness and mindfulness.	The poem features a volta which makes a workable association and reflects a basic sense of awareness and/or mindfulness.	The poem does not feature a volta, or it features a volta that seems forced, clichéd, or artificial.
Imagery			
The poem's imagery is vivid, unexpected, and focused; the images seem to transcend singular meaning and taken on a multifaceted quality.	The poem's imagery is vivid and focused; the images begin to take on a multifaceted quality.	The poem's imagery is concrete if not vivid; the images have potential for multiple meanings.	The poem's imagery is abstract, lifeless, and banal. The meaning of said imagery appears forced or haphazard.

Haiku Exercise Grading Rubric			
Demonstrates Exceptional Proficiency (40 points)	Demonstrates Advanced Proficiency (30 points)	Demonstrates Basic Proficiency (20 points)	Needs Improvement (10 points)
Language			
The poem's language achieves a balance of richness and economy. It is musical, pleasantly rhythmic, and/ or offers a fresh understanding of familiar words.	The poem's language is musical, pleasantly rhythmic, and/or offers a fresh understanding of familiar words.	The poem's language is somewhat musical and/ or rhythmic. It may offer a fresh understanding of familiar words.	The poem's language lacks melodic and/ or rhythmic qualities.
Form			
The poem's lines are intricately crafted, with deliberate and skillful line breaks. The poem's brevity seems effortless and unaffected.	The poem's lines are well crafted, with deliberate line breaks. The poem's brevity seems genuine.	The poem's lines are fairly well crafted, with deliberate line breaks. The poem's brevity may seem forced.	The poem's lines seem sloppily crafted, with uninteresting line breaks. The poem's brevity seems forced.

Typically, rubrics will describe the features of a high-scoring and low-scoring student for each criterion, and the instructor will indicate how the work has fared by marking the rubric accordingly, allowing the instructor to calculate a score, percentage, or letter grade. The rubric above lists four important criteria of a specific poetic form: a haiku. While these criteria are far from the final say on what it means to write successful haiku, they do represent some basic craft elements that students need to learn, hands-on, by writing this kind of poem. This rubric also wouldn't come to students out of the blue; I would have distributed it beforehand and discussed it with students, using examples and discussing my grading process. It's important to know that rubrics aren't arbitrary; instructors create summative evaluations like rubrics by researching the best examples of the work they're grading, then doing further research on how to teach students to produce such work. Far from being expressions of instructor opinion or a "fill-in-the-blank" exercise, rubrics reflect theoretical knowledge, careful analysis, and an understanding of how to teach.

Some other kinds of summative assignments in creative writing classes might include:

- individual creative pieces, such as a single poem or story;
- craft exercises, such as a poem written in a specific form;
- written responses to assigned readings;
- critical analysis papers, which may or may not include research;
- oral presentations of research or readings of creative work;
- written or oral exams;
- proposals for projects; and, of course,
- cumulative portfolios of creative work.

Just about any assignment in a creative writing class can be assigned a formal, summative grade. However, creative writing instructors don't always use rubrics. Offering rubrics might not align with a specific instructor's teaching philosophy, and the use of rubrics may or may not be encouraged by specific writing programs. There is a great deal of debate about the use of rubrics in all kinds of college writing classes. Some believe that rubrics are a vital tool for helping students and instructors understand and articulate the goals of learning, while others believe that rubrics can lead to stilted, formulaic writing with little originality and stylistic innovation.

In recent years, colleges and universities in North America have been encouraging more rigorous and frequent assessment of student learning on the programmatic or whole-college level. This means that programs that may never before have done the kinds of assessments common in K–12 education are now needing to provide evidence that their students are indeed learning what they need to learn. Creative writing programs are facing this shift, and faculty and administrators are finding that producing meaningful assessments is very complicated and challenging. This is why creative writing course syllabi are now starting to include very specific student learning outcomes, and why creative writing assignments are starting to come with attached grading rubrics. In the next section, we'll take a closer look at the variety of courses one might encounter in creative writing programs in North America, and how assignments in those courses are graded.

Creative Writing Courses: Curricula, Assignments, Grades
No matter what type, level, or format of creative writing program you might find yourself investigating, you'll

encounter a few standard types of courses: workshop courses, craft courses, professionalization courses, and pedagogy courses. While some creative writing programs require more types of courses than these four listed (literature survey courses or composition courses, for example), I will focus on these courses as they are specific to creative writing and compose the most common kinds of creative writing program curricula in colleges and universities in North America. For each kind of course, I will offer a brief description of its curriculum, mention a few assignments you're likely to encounter, and describe how the course is typically graded.

WORKSHOP COURSES

The *workshop course* is the course most common in creative writing programs. Writing workshops are collaborative sessions in which creative work is critiqued by both experienced and novice artists (Bishop and Starkey 2006). They are arguably the oldest established type of creative writing course in North America, and are commonly traced to the Iowa Writers' Workshop at the University of Iowa. In 1930, the Iowa Writers' Workshop began awarding MFA degrees in creative writing, and since then has employed some of the most high-profile writers in America as instructors, and has itself produced an impressive roster of prize-winning writers (Bishop and Starkey 2006). While the Iowa Writers' Workshop—and the workshop format itself—has faced criticism over the years, the "Iowa method" workshop continues to be the most common collaborative activity creative writers engage in, and it is not likely to leave the university any time soon.

In a workshop course, the workshop format itself is the centerpiece of course content and will usually guide instruction and any assignments given. Students turn in creative pieces weekly or every few weeks, and the majority of class time is spent critiquing and discussing the creative pieces that are "up" for that particular session. Instructors usually require that students comment in some way on others' creative drafts, and may collect them to analyze and evaluate student feedback; in a workshop, it's just as important to learn to give honest and constructive feedback to others as it is to graciously accept such feedback on your own work.

In terms of graded work, the workshop is usually very idiosyncratic and dependent on the preferences of the instructor or program. Your grade may be determined from some combination of attendance, active participation, insightful peer feedback, and your process of submitting, revising, polishing, and reflecting on your own creative work via a final portfolio or collection. Sometimes instructors include components such as discussion leading, reading logs, exercises, presentations, and even brief papers or reports in workshop classes. Generally, though, longer research papers are rarely assigned; these papers are much more likely to appear in a second type of creative writing course which I will discuss next—a craft course.

Craft Courses

The second most common type of course found in creative writing programs is the *craft course*, which are those courses that aim to teach some particular aspect of the writer's craft. Craft can be defined as the writer's technique of achieving desired artistic effects, and although some writers and teachers have noted that this definition doesn't encompass everything that "craft" can and should be (Mayers 2005), it remains the clearest way to distinguish the content of the craft course from other courses. Craft courses aim to hone your skill with specific techniques, styles, and genres of writing. In terms of format, these courses are rich in variety, but they usually involve some combination of instructor lecture, reading from published texts, whole-group and/or small-group discussion or in-class activities, short graded and/or ungraded writing exercises or assignments, longer graded papers or projects, and oral presentations or readings. Under the umbrella of craft courses, I am also including courses that might be called "genre courses," "form and/or theory courses," or "studio courses." That is because these courses differ enough from the standard workshop course to be considered in a second category, and because all of these courses are in some way designed to increase your knowledge—functional or critical—of particular aspects of the craft of writing. As a graduate student, I took a course called "Theory of Poetry;" this course was required as part of my creative writing degree although we close-read a selection of Modernist poems instead of writing our own. Although I didn't hand in any creative work to that professor that semester, I learned a great deal about sound, rhythm, and economy of language that enhanced the poetry I wrote later on.

In a "Craft of Poetry" course, you might have a unit in which you work with line breaks: you would read and discuss poems focusing on enjambment, and your instructor might give you a number of writing exercises designed to help you deploy line breaks effectively and in a style unique to you. A "Craft of Nonfiction" course might include a unit on epistolary essays, in which you might be required to emulate the letter-essay form used by Virginia Woolf. You're increasingly likely to encounter a large variety of fiction craft courses, some focused on writing popular genres: you might find yourself in a "Craft of Science Fiction" course, tackling a writing prompt about a new technology or the consequences of time travel. As usual, in all of these courses, grading is explained in a syllabus and instructors are required to make their expectations for successful assignments known in some way, even if they don't use rubrics.

PROFESSIONALIZATION COURSES

A third type of course that is becoming more and more popular in creative writing programs today is the *professionalization course.* In this kind of course, you can expect to learn something about what it means to be a writer in the "real world," often by working with editors, publishers, or arts organizations. A typical professionalization course might be a for-credit internship with an established literary journal, where students would gain experience reading submissions, writing reviews, judging contests, and perhaps even learning document design and social media marketing. In another course, students might be responsible for developing a literary blog, launching a reading series, or planning a conference. Some programs offer a professionalization course called a "literary citizenship" course in which students are invited to consider the landscape of creative writing and how it is affected by changes in culture, politics, and technology.

In professionalization courses, the classroom may be the office of a literary press or the production room of a journal, and instructors may shift to a "coaching" role while allowing students to design their own projects. Graded work in these courses often looks identical to "real world" work; students might hand in such things as query letters, book reviews, and blog posts that are meticulously edited and ready for literary audiences. Reflective writing is often a central part of professionalization courses, as students are invited to consider how the course and its assignments have affected the way they perceive the life and world of the creative writer.

PEDAGOGY COURSES

A final type of creative writing course is one that is likely not available to you as an undergraduate; nevertheless, it is highly important and is nearly always part of a graduate creative writing curriculum. This is the *pedagogy course.* The word "pedagogy" refers to the theory and practice of teaching, and thus a creative writing pedagogy course would teach students how to teach creative writing to others. In North America, creative writing pedagogy courses have existed in some form or another for at least as long as creative writing programs have existed, and they have been the subject of much spirited debate as the theories and assumptions behind them have grown and changed (in fact, in the early days of creative writing programs, the party line was that creative writing could *not* be taught; see D.G. Myers' 1996 history of creative writing programs, *The Elephants Teach,* for more on that debate). In pedagogy courses, students learn both the theory and practice of teaching creative writing via readings and discussion, writing research papers, creating classroom materials such as syllabi and lesson plans, grading student assignments, and observing and teaching actual creative writing classes. Additionally, students in these courses will usually have their teaching observed by the instructor at least once. After that observation, the instructor will share feedback with the student and highlight strong and weak points of the observed teaching. The instructor will likely then ask the student to reflect on the observation experience and develop a plan for improvement.

That most graduate creative writing programs now include a required creative writing pedagogy class is a testament to how important effective teaching has become in the professional lives of creative writers. Graduates may never teach in formal university or K–12 educational settings, but writers encounter countless festivals, residencies, artist colonies, community workshops, and private mentoring opportunities that can make use of pedagogical skills.

Conclusion: How to Use Grading to Grow as a Writer
By now, I hope that you've started to understand grading a bit better, and that you've come to see why well-reasoned assessment is an essential component of legitimate, credential-bestowing creative writing programs in North America today. In fact, there's a lot more to this subject than what I've outlined in this chapter—papers and articles and books worth. But in closing this particular piece of writing, I'd like to offer you a few recommendations for how to use what you've learned about grading to enhance your student creative-writing experience.

START A CONVERSATION WITH YOUR INSTRUCTORS,
PROGRAM ADMINISTRATORS, AND FELLOW STUDENTS
It's not uncommon for some creative writing instructors (and even for some students) to feel that grading is an inappropriate topic of discussion. Remember, too, that most instructors have at times had unpleasant experiences when discussing grading with students and administrators, and may be hesitant or even defensive when the subject

comes up. If you want to talk about grading, be gentle, respectful, and persistent. Approach your instructors and fellow students with an attitude of friendly curiosity instead of confrontation. You will find that a good conversation about grading can be illuminating and encouraging.

LEARN HOW YOU'LL BE GRADED, AND FIND WAYS TO
MEASURE YOUR GROWTH ASIDE FROM GRADES
As noted in this chapter, there are still many instructors who believe that creative writing cannot and should not be graded, and thus may have their own idiosyncratic practices when it comes time to mark the report cards. However, there are just as many instructors who lay out their grading practices in great detail. In any case, you should carefully read information about grading in program documents, student handbooks, syllabuses, assignment sheets, and other class materials, and (politely!) ask questions when things aren't clear. You should also ask how instructors will measure your growth as a writer in more nuanced ways. Grades, as they say, are a blunt instrument; a letter or score can't replace the timely, carefully-worded feedback that writers rely on to improve. Ask your creative writing instructors for the opportunity to talk about your writing without the worry of grading. They'll be happy to see that your investment in their courses goes beyond your GPA.

RECOGNIZE THAT THE DEBATES ABOUT GRADING AND
CREATIVE WRITING HAVE BARELY EVEN BEGUN
Remind yourself that while grading is well established in American higher education, grading creative writing is much more changeable terrain. Right now, a growing number of students, instructors, scholars, and administrators are

102

asking new questions and conducting new research about this topic; they're considering the impacts of such issues as identity, difference, economics, and technology on how students are evaluated and how curriculums are assessed. What this means is that grading in creative writing is likely to become a conversation in which you can take part, and even have an impact on. Imagine if you could empower yourself and your fellow students by working hand-in-hand with instructors and administrators in setting goals and establishing benchmarks, and discovering new, more equitable ways to define success. Wouldn't you emerge from that experience a stronger, wiser, more seasoned writer? I know I would.

Chapter Nine

Learning Creative Writing in Cyberspace: Getting the Most out of an Online Creative Writing Course

JOSEPH REIN

To begin, a confession: I am no technology expert. In some ways, I'm the least tech-savvy person I know. I don't have a Facebook or Twitter account. I just recently purchased my first smartphone, and not entirely by choice. My computer exists mainly to word process and email. My own children get a set amount of screen time during the day, and I often worry about the growing number of us who spend more time logged in than living.

And yet, with all that said, I have come to love online courses. When done well, these courses take advantage of all the great benefits technology can afford. They make the inclusion of video, audio, and other media a snap. They also create a deep well of information from which we can pull at any time. And, perhaps most importantly, they fit the lifestyle of the contemporary college student, whose circumstances may make traditional classroom attendance next to impossible.

Looking back on the early years of my online instruction, this last notion excited me the most: *I can set my own schedule! I can teach in my pajamas!* And to some extent, this excitement has yet to wane. I've taught online creative writing courses for nearly ten years now, and each one teaches me something new as well: something about myself, my teaching style, or even my own writing.

In those ten years, however, I've also discovered the most crucial aspect of online courses: they are more difficult to execute successfully, both from my standpoint as a professor and yours as a student. Many people presume that online classes will be less work than their face-to-face counterparts. This couldn't be further from the truth, a fact to which anyone who has either taught or taken an online course can attest. My early students consistently remarked as much in their end-of-class evaluations, and so now I begin every online course as I now begin this essay: *Taking a course online will be a good deal more work than you're expecting.*

However, that fact shouldn't deter anyone, particularly us creative writers. After all, we are conditioned to write between classes and homework, after nightfall or before daybreak, in the small gaps of our lives. Also, as I outline below, knowing the key components of the course and how best to navigate them will ensure that the hard work you invest will, by the end of the course and beyond, pay great dividends.

Online Citizenship

Imagine yourself stepping into a traditional classroom on the first day. You find a place to sit. You pull out a pen and paper. You wave to or chat with those you know. You play on your phone. And finally the clock ticks down to your start time, when your professor hands out a syllabus and begins explaining the course rules which, for the remainder of the semester, you will follow.

For me, this situation happens a half dozen or more times a year. And though the first day is not often the most exciting, it serves a very crucial function that online courses have a hard time recreating. The first day of class is comfortable, familiar. We all know what we're going to get. We find out what our professor expects of us, and we learn what we must do to be successful. But online, even if we're familiar with our university's course management system—yours may be Blackboard, Moodle, D2L Brightspace or something similar—the unfamiliarity with the professor, your classmates, the course content itself, can often leave you feeling lost. *What am I supposed to do?* you might ask. Or more importantly, *How am I supposed to act?*

Though it might seem like a free-for-all at first, codes of conduct still exist for each online classroom, and familiarizing yourself with and following these codes will ultimately lead you to a more successful and enriching experience. I will start here with the most basic, and work toward more creative-writing-specific topics. Of course, each professor will have her own guidelines to follow, and those trump any suggestions I pose here. But like your professor's guidelines, my suggestions are far from arbitrary; in many cases I arrived at them only after a good deal of trial-and-error, through the inevitable knowledge gained from repeated experience.

Be "Present"

I start here because, in many ways, this is your most important task in an online course. In a face-to-face classroom, I can physically see you attend, participate, engage. Just being in your seat—having a specific place at all—and listening attentively, you assure your presence in class. Online, from behind a computer screen, this is much harder to do.

Becoming actively involved is step number one. This seems easy enough, until you take into account the aforementioned workload you might find thrust upon you. The key is to budget yourself daily time for your online course. In online courses, many professors will allow you to hand in assignments later in the day, or even at midnight of the given due date. Here, the flexibility—the ability to work when you can, not on a set schedule—is one of the real benefits. But if you don't carve out specific time for the course, it can easily become an afterthought, a missed step, a website you don't check for days. That's when you'll find yourself behind.

One part here bears repeating: *daily* time. Some professors will contact you if you "go missing" for a few days, but others—like myself—feel it is your responsibility to keep in contact with the course. So make a habit of checking your online classroom, however you can best remind yourself. Bookmark the page, leave a sticky note on your laptop, set a daily reminder alarm on your phone. Make it habitual, the same way you might check Facebook or email or favorite websites. Add it to the stop list on your metaphorical internet train ride.

This also brings to light the issue of *synchronous vs. asynchronous* communication, a common issue in online instruction. The concepts themselves are quite simple: synchronous communication means that two or more people are communicating simultaneously, in the same space. This can include anything from chat spaces to online classrooms to conference calls (like Skype, FaceTime, or Hangout). Asynchronous communication means that communication happens at any given time, depending on when the participants choose to engage in it. This communication happens via online discussion boards, Tweets, Facebook messages. The simplest example is phone calls vs. text messages: although both are communication, calls are synchronous while texts are asynchronous.

In my experience, most professors lean toward asynchronous communication for a number of reasons. We understand that you often take online courses because of your limited availability. I am currently teaching an online course in which one student works three jobs outside school, another watches his five children, and another resides in London. This is one aspect that makes online instruction exciting: the great diversity of students. In creative writing especially, online courses make for some of the best, most varied, and intriguing writing situations. We learn from each other, and myriad world experiences can only help. But having those same three students come together simultaneously on a regular basis can be difficult, if not impossible.

It's important to be aware of the expectations for participation in your online course, be it synchronous or asynchronous. Ultimately, the responsibility to be *present* in class lies more heavily on your shoulders in the online sphere. Though your professor may give you more freedom to work on your own time, this also means you'll have limited opportunities to show your engagement in the course. So take advantage when you can: an extra post here, or a lively conversation in the chat room there, can go a long way.

But posting is not the only way to show presence in your course. Like in face-to-face classrooms, attending and listening can have a profound effect on your learning, not to mention your grade. Simply viewing all course content—lectures, videos, posts from your professor and classmates—will demonstrate your online presence. Here's how: in online courses, professors can track your activity in your online classroom. So, for example, if you watch a lecture video or read a discussion post, your professor has access to data that will tell her when exactly this happens. This will give her an accurate idea of how engaged you may be in the course, simply by knowing whether you've accessed the content.

I tell you this not to frighten you, to give you the Big-Brother sense that "you're being watched." I joke with colleagues of a hypothetical professor awake at all hours behind a glowing computer screen, hair frazzled, endless mug of coffee in hand, a finger constantly refreshing his browser to check if any students have recently watched a lecture. This just doesn't happen. Many professors, like myself, do not view such data in order to gauge the popularity of our posts (akin to Tweets or Facebook status updates). Nor do we view the data in order to create a hierarchy in the course, to exalt the engaged and outcast the disengaged. In reality, I look at this data sparingly, and only as a reward for participation. In some ways, this feature is simply the equivalent of attendance in class, and I encourage you to think of it that way. As difficult as it can be to engage the course material if you never attend class, it can be doubly difficult if you don't follow the professor's daily activities, watch videos, read lectures, post on discussion boards: in short, if you're not *present.*

Overall, your success in the course will depend on your conscious efforts to become involved. Though it is a cliché, in online classes it's also terrifically true: you get what you give.

The Online Workshop (or, Respecting Your Classmates)
In creative writing, most peer-to-peer communication happens through "workshop." Basically, you will present work for critique, and will be presented with your peers'

work as well. Most of your communication for this will likely happen through discussion boards, which asynchronously replicate a workshop setting. Depending on the course, your responses to your classmates may constitute a good amount of your grade, so learning quickly how to best compose these responses will be critical to your success.

TONE

I'll begin my discussion of tone, as I often do in my fiction-writing class, with a question: what exactly is it? How do we identify it? When my students reference a writer's tone in discussion, I quickly ask them to point out a specific moment: where do we see the writer's self-reflective or sophisticated or angry tone? In the end, it all boils down to the language the writer uses, to his words and the way he constructs them. So saying "flummoxed" presents sophistication, whereas "pissed off" shows harshness. Length of sentences, diction, syntax: we pay attention to these in our own creative works to carefully construct the tone we wish to convey. And often, the strongest tones in writing feature bold, distinct choices that set the writing apart from the rest.

But in responses to each other, for some reason, being bold in our tone often has negative consequences. Our tone and meaning, often inflected by our personalities, can become skewed in the online sphere. Sarcasm, for example, is very hard to gauge on the screen. What you perceive as a simple joke quickly becomes hurtful to the recipient. An excess of tone—exclamation marks for example—can make a straightforward comment such as *The imagery could be stronger* an affront.

This doesn't mean, however, that you need be entirely straightforward with your comments, or that you should eliminate your personality. It simply means that, like any written communication, you need to be aware that the way you intend something to sound may not be the way it is received.

There are easy counteractions to this, however. Because you have time to construct your feedback, you should take the extra steps to make it clear. Using "I-centered" language instead of "you-centered" language is a start. Doing so places you as a reader, with one interpretation, rather than an editor insisting upon change. For example, saying, *I thought the dialogue on page two was a bit flat,* will probably be much better received than something like, *You should change the flat dialogue on page two.* They are essentially the same comment with changes in tone. Of course, at times it will make more sense to make direct suggestions to the writer. In those cases, try to offer your comments as possibilities (*you might*) instead of necessities (*you need to*).

Finally, sometimes it can be as simple as rereading your critique before posting. Ask yourself: *How would I receive this feedback? Would I be hurt or offended if someone said this to me?* Or read it to a friend, asking her the same questions. Though goodwill is often assumed online, it can also be easily lost, and the extra minute it takes to carefully consider your interactions with others will go miles toward good online citizenship.

SPECIFICITY

An equally important part of your posts, which is my number one rule in giving feedback: be specific. For example, telling a classmate that her characters really shined might boost her confidence, but it likely will not lead to growth, in the piece or otherwise. It leads her to questions like, *Which characters? All of them? Does that mean I shouldn't work on characterization at all?* A much stronger, and more specific, response might say: *I really enjoyed the character of Vince. He's lively, described in great physical detail, and has an irresistible charm about him.* Even better, you might point to specific passages or lines about Vince that stood out to you as particularly strong. Doing so shows your investment in, and thorough consideration of, your classmates' work, and encourages them to reciprocate.

"REPLY TO ALL"

Dialogue is essential to good online communication. Think of those times in class when everyone seems to be talking *at* instead of *with* each other: each speaker introduces a new idea that seems disconnected from the previous; trains of thought get lost almost before they arrive; many speak but few listen. This is an easy trap to fall into online, especially if you haven't read or considered previous posts.

In a face-to-face workshop, the immediacy of the moment allows us to follow trends in the comments, to add or detract, to compliment or refute a specific point: in other words, to have a dialogue. This can be replicated online, but it takes a conscientious effort. You must reply to the work, but also to the other voices in the room as well. It's helpful to think of the email analogy of *Reply* against *Reply to All*. If you hit *Reply*, then you respond just to the initial writer of the email. If, however, you *Reply to All*, you now send something that needs to address the entire conversation. For example: a friend emails you asking about possible weekend plans. In a *Reply* situation, you simply write back with a list of ideas. But now imagine that friend has emailed five other people as well, and three have already replied. To reply only to the initial question may help; if anything, your friend can tally votes. However, more useful would be a response that picks up where the conversation left off. This way, the conversation becomes a continuum, a progression from the last point as opposed to a constant reset back to the opening.

In creative writing, the *Reply* situation can be frustrating. Hearing the same point over and over is less beneficial than hearing that same point expanded upon, altered, or even refuted. Reading all previous posts, and considering them as you write your own, will help your class create the dialogue necessary to a great workshop experience.

Receiving Feedback (or, Respecting Your Professor)
In your creative writing course, you will receive as much feedback—if not more—than you give. At first glance, it might seem like receiving feedback needs little suggestion: don't you just read, absorb, and then revise? Well, yes and no. In my experience, receiving feedback can be just as much a skill as giving it. After all, what you do with your feedback—how you use it to improve your work—may be the most important part of your education as a writer

First, I always tell students to hope for—but not expect—a thorough, thoughtful critique every time. At times, your classmates or professor may not have fully understood your work, or may not have invested as much time in it as you'd like. And yes, we would all appreciate deep, helpful, positive and yet constructive feedback every time we write a new piece. In an ideal world, your professor at least will provide this every time. But it's important to remember that she is human, and likes to see her hard work pay off too. In other words, if she spends the better part of an afternoon providing detailed, critical feedback to a class of twenty, and then sees only four of those students actually read that feedback, she may feel disheartened. She may feel much less inclined to spend the time or go as in-depth on the next assignment. (You may find yourself feeling the same way if you spend significantly more time on your feedback than your classmates.)

Thus, showing your professor your serious investment in the work of the course will only enhance her willingness to offer you deep, sustained feedback. My students often contact me for extra discussion on their work, but afterwards, they will apologize: *Sorry to bother you,* they say, or worse, *I don't want to waste your time.* I always stop them and tell them never to apologize. Having engaged, enthused students who care about their work makes my job worthwhile. So don't be afraid to ask follow-ups to your professor's feedback, or engage her in discussions on your work, or on writing in general. I promise you: it's these moments for which we teach.

MODE OF COMMUNICATION

In our day-to-day life, we generally take our myriad forms of communication for granted. We have email accounts, social media sites, video messaging services, phones: and that's all beyond face-to-face conversations. When viewed in a positive light, we see abundance, options. We can talk to someone in so many ways. But in our online classes, this plethora can cause information to get lost in the digital ether. The question comes to me often: *Did you get my email?* I've gotten it so often, in fact, that it has become my personal motto for this uncertainty, this challenge we face in corresponding in such a variety of ways.

Online courses move quickly, so an unanswered or lost email can get you behind just as fast. Though you might not avoid this completely, you can also minimize the chances by communicating with your professor in the way in which she communicates with you. For example, if your professor sends course correspondence through email, then feel free to email her with questions. However, if she has set up a specific place in your online classroom for correspondence, then your emails may not be as effective. I've seen many instances where such questions were lost or simply buried beneath other correspondence. Finding the direct path to communication with your professor will lessen the chances of missed communication.

Also, attempt to find answers yourself before contacting your professor. Check your syllabus, course website, previous correspondence. If you ask too many questions with apparent answers— *When is this assignment due? How many words should this be?*—you may receive any array of responses, from a helpful answer to a simple, *Check your syllabus.* You can, of course, ask clarifying questions if things are unclear. As a professor, it can be difficult to gauge whether I've described something in enough detail. For every online class, I set up a discussion thread for such technical or logistical issues, and I prefer having students ask there, since everyone can see it. But asking questions that I've addressed elsewhere displays a lack of engagement with the material, and makes me feel as though my work put into the course is not being fully respected.

Final Thoughts

In my years of teaching online courses, I find distance to be the largest obstacle we face: distance from campus, from the course material, from one another. Online communities can and do thrive, but they take an extra step, an added awareness, a more conscientious effort on everyone's part. The concepts I present here are not novel to college classrooms: presence, respect, open communication. The same precepts will make you successful online as well, with a few alterations of course. And as universities become increasingly reliant on technology, computers, the internet—as we become increasingly online—those who recognize these alterations, will thrive, will grow as writers, and will ultimately find themselves at the head of the digital class.

Chapter Ten

Beyond Graduation: Sustaining Yourself as a Writer

ANNA LEAHY

By the time you finish your program in creative writing, you will have learned a lot about writing: how reading can inform and widen your choices as a writer, how to recognize the strengths and weaknesses in your drafts, how to revise, and even how your habits and interests fuel or distract you from your work. If you've planned well, as Stephanie Vanderslice suggested in the first chapter of this book, you know these things as skills, in ways that apply specifically to you and your writing process, but also in more general ways that might lead to and be used for a paying job.

One of my college friends wrote for a greeting card company. Another wrote for and edited publications at a company that manufactured large farm equipment. Scott Turow was a practicing lawyer for years, drafting his novels on his commute to and from work. Nina Corwin is a psychotherapist, Victoria Chang is a businessperson, and Stephanie Brown and Nancy Kuhl are librarians—they've all published poetry books. As poet Richard Hugo wrote in *The Triggering Town,* "no job accounts for the impulse to find and order those bits and pieces of yourself that can come out only in the most unguarded moments, in the wildest, most primitive phrases we shout alone at the mirror. And no job modifies that impulse or destroys it"

(p. 109). Regardless of what else you do with your time and your life, a writer writes.

On *The Daily Show*, novelist John Irving said that an MFA—a Master of Fine Arts—saved him time, and that's a good way to think of any writing program, graduate or undergraduate. A degree in creative writing is a means to help you become the best writer you can be more quickly and to jump-start a writing life that you'll need to sustain on your own over the long haul. Graduation may end your college career, but it is the beginning of the next stage of your writing life.

After you graduate, mentors and peers who *get* what you're doing won't be right around the corner, and recommended readings, prompts, and deadlines will disappear. That change may feel like a relief and freedom for some. As Natalie Goldberg wrote in *Writing Down the Bones*, "I was not in school anymore: I could say what I wanted" (p. 2). But the flipside of this freedom is that you'll have to figure out for yourself how to keep writing, improve as a writer, and publish your work.

Not every graduate of a creative writing program does this. In fact, many leave creative writing behind as they build their lives around other pursuits. Of course, a person can come back to writing later in life, and some successful writers didn't start writing and publishing seriously until they'd racked up accomplishments in other areas. Laura Ingalls Wilder started writing in her mid-forties and didn't publish her first book until she was sixty-four years old. Toni Morrison wrote her first novel at age thirty-nine. Often, the late bloomer has been practicing the craft a long time. In an article in *The New Yorker*, Malcolm Gladwell pointed to research by David Galenson that lyric poets tend to write plenty of good work after age fifty and pointed to the example of novelist Ben Fountain, who got his big break at age forty-eight, after eighteen years of serious writing.

This chapter is designed especially for those students who want to sustain their writing lives from the get-go and stick with it to see how things pan out.

How Important Is Your Writing?

Students finishing up a program in creative writing are in a great position to think about ways to continue the habits that the program cultivated. It's inherently a fresh start, but, without the structure of a creative writing program, the individual has to create a day-to-day life in which writing matters.

In *Steal Like an Artist,* erasure poet and self-made creativity expert Austin Kleon says:

> I'm a boring guy with a nine-to-five job who lives in a quiet neighborhood with his wife and his dog. That whole romantic image of the creative genius doing drugs and running around and sleeping with everyone is played out. It's for the superhuman and the people who want to die young. The thing is: It takes a lot of energy to be creative. You don't have that energy if you waste it on other stuff. (Kleon, p. 119)

If writing is important to you, if it brings you joy even as it challenges you, if you want to call yourself a writer, you need to make choices about how you expend your energy and time.

Several years ago, for instance, my husband and I gave up television to shift from viewing habits to writing habits. We signed up for Netflix but limited ourselves to two discs by mail. That's right, no streaming; we can't watch whatever we want whenever we want to watch it. Our friends and family think we're living in the dark ages, but we've written more in the dark.

Where does writing rank in your life? Is it more or less important than other things you have to do or want to do? How urgent does it feel it to you? And what do you want to accomplish with that urgency?

In order to establish writing habits, it helps to set goals. Setting goals can be a quandary for any writer, but especially for an emerging writer. After all, I may want to write the next great American novel, but I have control over only part of that process and phenomenon. So my goals need to reflect the accomplishments I can achieve myself: writing chapter after chapter, revising and revising again, reading to think about how novels work, getting feedback and revising again, and querying agents.

What is it you want to accomplish as a writer? Think big. Think long term. Be specific. It's unlikely that an emerging poet without a book will place a poem at *The Atlantic,* but that's a goal that might keep a person writing, submitting work to literary journals, and building a book manuscript. Learning everything you can this year about voice in nonfiction is another type of big, specific goal. Think about goals you can set that encourage accomplishment along the way to build momentum. Think about projects big enough that they can be broken into smaller parts. In an interview with Oprah Winfrey, novelist Cormac McCarthy said, "You always have the image of the perfect thing, which you can never achieve but which you never stop trying to achieve." When you think of what you want to accomplish as a writer, don't be afraid to set a goal or imagine a project that seems beyond what you know you can finish in the next week or month. Even if you don't accomplish that goal, you'll learn and produce a lot along the way.

Recently, *The ONE Thing* by Gary Keller reminded me of some of these ways of thinking about the writing life. That book emphasizes that those aspects of life most important to you should get the most time and energy. I've read similar advice and research dozens of times before, but I need to remind myself and be reminded that multitasking is not effective. Focus matters to a writer. Though Keller's book is not directed toward writers per se, another of its points is that a balanced life, at least day to day or hour to hour, is a myth for high achievers:

> When you act on your priority, you'll automatically go out of balance, giving more time to one thing than another. [...] The challenge becomes how long you stay on your priority. [...] When you're supposed to be working, work, and when you're supposed to be playing, play. (p. 82)

No one *has* to write a poem or the next great American novel, so if you choose to write a poem, you're choosing to not spend that time and energy on something else. That's not to say that writing is the only thing in your life that's important but that, if writing is important to you, then, when you write, that must be your focus.

On Time and Timing

In a piece for *Minerva Rising*, I wrote, "*I'll make time* is a lie we tell ourselves. Time cannot be created. There are two common ways of perceiving time: either we are rushing headlong into the future, or the future is rushing headlong toward us. Either way, there will exist only 24 hours in each day." Writers who sit around trying to make or find time are fooling themselves. Instead, we must look at the 24 hours we have each day, recognize how we are spending them, and make sure that writing gets the time it deserves based on how important it is in our lives. That's not easy, even for those of us who've been writing for decades.

Some writers don't write every day, but many of those who don't wish they did. It's common sense that practice-based tasks—yoga, playing an instrument, writing—are most beneficial and show improvement when done with regularity. Novelist Walter Mosley, in his book *This Year You Write Your Novel*, advises:

> The first thing you have to know about writing is that it is something you must do every day—every morning or every night, whatever time it is that you have. Ideally, the time you decide on is also the time when you do your best work. There are two reasons for this rule: getting the work done and connecting with your unconscious mind. (p. 7)

In other words, make writing an artistic practice instead of merely another item on a list of things to do.

Habits require time and repetition. In *The ONE Thing*, Gary Keller points to research that suggests "it takes an average of 66 days to acquire a new habit" but admits it might take four times as long as that (p. 59). In thinking about writing as a practice, Natalie Goldberg compares writing to running:

> You practice whether you want to or not. You don't wait around for inspiration and a deep desire to run. It'll never happen,

especially if you are out of shape and have been avoiding it. But if you run regularly, you train your mind to cut through or ignore your resistance. You just do it. (p. 11)

The writing habit becomes part of the writer's mindset, which is especially important when the external prompts and deadlines of a creative writing program aren't there.

In addition, regular practice embeds some aspects of writing deeply, like the muscle memory of a baseball player who no longer has to consciously think about his stance or timing of his swing. As Richard Hugo puts it,

> if I seem to talk technique now and then and urge you to learn more, it is not so you will remember it when you write but so you can forget it. Once you have a certain accumulated technique, you can forget it in the act of writing. Those moves that are naturally yours will stay with you and will come forth mysteriously when needed. (p. 17)

Writers learn by writing, by *doing*.

Every writer must determine when to write. Say you follow Mosley's recommendation. You may think you know when that is, but have you tested different writing times for a couple of weeks? Or have you written only when you felt like it and assumed that you felt like it because you could do your best work then?

Keller recommends doing the most important thing—in our case, writing—first, before your willpower is taxed by other tasks (pp. 65–71). I'm not a morning person and often feel as if I have more energy later in the day, but even before I read *The ONE Thing,* I tried writing before everything else because I'd heard about research that supported the idea. After breakfast but before email, texting, grading, or meetings, I wrote. I had to admit that I focused better early in the day, before I became involved mentally in other tasks. And I produced more writing over time because, when I wrote early, other tasks couldn't squeeze writing out of a day's schedule.

In addition to committing to when you will write, you also need to decide how long you will write. There exist two basic options: either you set a word or page count, or you set a timer. If you're working on a novel, for instance, you could set a goal of writing one page per day and have a complete draft in a year. Natalie Goldberg says, "My rule is to finish a notebook a month" (p. 11). Maybe you want to write and revise one poem each week, or maybe you want to write and revise one essay each month.

Goldberg, though, is ultimately an advocate of timed writing. Keller goes further to recommend time blocking—putting when and how long on your calendar along with *everything* else—in part because research by K. Anders Ericsson, which was popularized by Malcolm Gladwell, suggests that mastery requires 10,000 hours of practice (p. 177). Let's say you commit to writing for 90 minutes a day 6 days a week, or 9 hours per week. That's 468 hours every year, so, at that pace, it'll take you more than 20 years to achieve mastery. As a creative writing student, you've already put in some of those hours, but think about what this math means to how you schedule your writing practice. Don't let that number intimidate you. Instead, think of every hour you spend writing as important because it adds up over time. Every hour is necessary, so you need to get started, and you need to keep going.

Mystery writer Elizabeth George puts it a slightly different way: "he who possesses the best bum glue wins"

(p. 190). In other words, the writer who spends the most time with his or her bum—or butt—in the chair doing the writing is more likely to become a successful, published writer. Find a good writing chair, and sit in it.

George adds, "bum glue is about commitment on every level: to the self, to the dream, and to the process" (p. 196). If you call yourself a writer—if that's who you are and what you want to be—you must do the writing. With a schedule that becomes a habit, you will do the writing, and you'll probably feel pretty good about it overall.

The Role of Connection

Writing is done in isolation and requires the individual writer's effort. Psychologist Nancy Andreasen, however, asserts, "It is more difficult for the creative brain to prosper in isolation" (p. 128). Her research indicates, "creative people are likely to be more productive and more original if surrounded by other creative people. This too produces an environment in which the creative brain is stimulated to form novel connections and novel ideas" (p. 129). A creative writing program surrounds individuals with other creative writers. After you graduate, you should consider the benefits, as a writer, of staying in touch with some of those fellow writers and of engaging with other creative people.

A writing group that meets regularly and expects every member to produce work for discussion is probably akin to workshops in which you've participated as a student. You may find or create a writing group on your own or through your local public library. The simplest, surest way to create such a group, however, is by gathering a few (but probably not more than five or six) like-minded (but critical) peers with whom you've already been in a workshop and whose commitment to writing is already established. The group may want to agree that every participant must share a certain number of pages for every gathering and will need to decide whether to share and read that work before meeting. Writer Anne Lamott recommends this sort of extension of the formal writing workshop or conference in her book *Bird by Bird,* not only for continued critique but also to talk about the craft and process of writing generally and to help each other through rough patches and getting stuck. Meeting in person is probably ideal, but Skype, which can be used for free, or another format for exchange can work as well. Meeting regularly, say once a month, encourages everyone in the group to be accountable on a regular basis to each other as well as themselves.

An alternative way to accomplish accountability is to find just one writing friend, agree to a plan—maybe writing 90 minutes every day or drafting a poem every week—then text or email each other when that benchmark is met each day or week. Any writer who wants to cultivate a habit, is skimping on writing time, or is spinning wheels during that writing time should consider a simple, external structure to be accountable for the work. A writing group or a buddy can also encourage reading, either by informal discussion or an agreed assignment like in a book club.

Not all connections should be treated equally, however. There's a lot of buzz out there about the dangers of the internet, social media, and gaming. In his book *The Shallows,* Nicholas Carr claims, "We are welcoming frenziedness into our souls" (p. 222), and, in some ways, he's right. The internet can be a huge distraction for a writer, and if you're drafting or revising on your computer, it's right there at your fingertips. It's tempting to look up one thing you need to know for the story you're writing but then to let one thing lead to another and another and then tweet some tidbit. That's why programs exist to block your access to the internet for a period of time you pre-set, and many writers use one because it's a good way to stay focused and to avoid draining willpower. Scheduling social media time or separating social media to a different device than the one used for writing is another good idea for many writers. And don't forget the potential benefits of drafting by hand: you probably write more slowly by hand, taking more time to think; you probably revise not merely retype when you transition to a computer; and some researchers have surmised that handwriting taps the brain in ways that encourage learning (Klemm 2013).

That said, the internet is also a great way to seek out advice from blogs by writers and agents and to connect with other writers through social media groups. It's relatively easy to start a private blog or secret Facebook group just for your writing group, and plenty of public groups (and closed ones that you can request to join) exist for sharing your work and getting advice about submissions, querying, and pitching. *Writer's Digest* publishes a list of top websites for writers every year, *Poets & Writers* maintains a searchable database of literary journals, and the National Novel Writing Month has a website to support participants in that project. As distracting as the internet can be, it's a great resource for answering questions, even questions you don't know to ask until you run across the answer.

Some of the ways you connect with other writers—recommending a book to a friend or publishing a book review, attending or hosting a reading, subscribing to and actually reading a literary journal to which you want to submit someday—will be a form of literary citizenship, which is the subject of the next chapter of this book. There, Donna Steiner points out that, by engaging in literary citizenship, "you will begin to actually live your beliefs and dreams." Connecting with other writers becomes an act of both selfishness and generosity, as you gain from the interactions and add to the community.

Whether and How to Continue Your Education

If you're a dedicated, growing writer and you want to become a professor of creative writing, you need a graduate degree to have a shot at one of the few positions that open up every year. Academic institutions require academic credentials for teaching positions, and the MFA usually qualifies in creative writing. A graduate degree, in and of itself, does not guarantee that a person will land a job as a professor. In fact, many academic positions either specifically require a book publication as well or the applicant pool is so promising that the search committee considers only those who have published a book. If your passion is teaching, you may want to consider getting certified to teach K–12, though that job has its own distinct qualifications and demands.

An MFA can help you become a better writer faster, though you don't need an MFA to become a successful writer. If you want to know more about MFA programs, both residential and low-residency, the Association of Writers and Writing Programs has a large, current, searchable list that covers "the United States and abroad." Some writers pursue an MFA because it fosters their development as an individual writer and as a part of a larger community of artists. Novelist and nonfiction writer Ann Patchett agrees: "This is where MFA programs are most valuable: you can learn more, and more quickly, from other people's missteps than from their successes. [...] Making friends with other writers you respect is reason enough to go to graduate school" (p. 36). I decided to earn an MFA because I wanted an additional two years of intensive reading and writing practice under the guidance of terrific mentors and in the company of talented peers. I learned a lot and have no regrets, and, when I finished my MFA, I became a production editor for science journals, in part because I had worked to develop my editing skills cultivated as an undergraduate.

Though some students or their families can pay for a graduate degree out of their own pockets, I would not have pursued an MFA without a teaching assistantship that included a full tuition waiver and a stipend. In addition, I had roommates to share rent costs, held a part-time job at a nearby mall, and took out student loans, which I only recently finished paying off. It's important to note that student loan rules have changed so that, unlike me, today's graduate students start accruing interest the day they get the federal student loan instead of six months after graduation. Ann Patchett, who earned an MFA at the Iowa Writers' Workshop, bluntly advises (p. 37), "no one should go into debt to study creative writing. It's simply not worth it. Do not think of it as an investment in yourself that you'll be able to recoup later on. [...] If you get into an MFA program without an offer of financial aid, sit out a year and reapply." Unless you're independently wealthy or the program caters to part-time students with full-time jobs, that's good advice. Low-residency programs, for instance, don't have teaching assistantships but are designed for people who have full-time jobs or cannot move to pursue a degree. For most writers, the MFA itself must be its own reward.

After finishing my MFA and working for a year as an editor, I entered a PhD program because I thought it would be like an MFA, only twice as long. But my PhD program was a much clearer commitment to and immersion in an academic career. That focus and depth as well as the additional teaching experience turned out to work well for me, but even PhD graduates have a tough time landing a tenure-track position. It took me more than a decade and several moves and jobs before I became a tenured professor at an up-and-coming university in California, far from where I'd ever lived before.

An MFA is great for some people, and I write letters of recommendation for several graduating seniors every year. That said, writers who want additional guidance don't have to pursue a graduate degree. One-off workshops and conferences can give your writing life a boost, and some offer financial support for participation. These opportunities are short-term commitments—a weekend, a week, sometimes a month—to nourish your writing self. I attend such a workshop or residency every few years. The Association of Writers and Writing Programs has a good, searchable *Directory of Conferences & Centers* that lists a variety of conferences, festivals, residencies, and retreats for writers. There exist such opportunities all over North America and beyond.

Your Writing Might Just Save the World
Anyone who completes a creative writing program knows what it takes to be a writer. The most important thing is to write and to organize one's life to encourage and

fuel that writing time. Maybe the issue is bigger than that. Novelist Margaret Atwood, in an article about a story-sharing platform (2012), makes the case for your work in the grand scheme of things: "Reading and writing, like everything else, improve with practice. And, of course, if there are no young readers and writers, there will shortly be no older ones. Literacy will be dead, and democracy—which many believe goes hand in hand with it—will be dead as well." Sustaining your own writing life may well be part of saving the world as we know it.

Chapter Eleven

Literary Citizenship: How You Can Contribute to the Literary Community and Why You Should

Donna Steiner

When I was in high school, the book *Howards End* by E.M. Forster was assigned in an English class. I was a good reader, but could not get into the novel. Every day I tried, but would stall quickly. I gave up.

Almost twenty years later I picked up the book again. I read it straight through, underlining passages, turning down corners of important pages. The story felt profound and resonant.

What changed in those years? Probably many things, but the bottom line was this: I was not ready for the novel in high school. Later, I was.

As a writer, when you are ready for something, you find it. Sometimes you find it right *before* you are ready, and find the courage to take that step even if it's nerve-wracking.

There are many steps we take as writers. The step this chapter will look at is called literary citizenship. Literary citizenship recognizes that we are all part of various writing communities, and supporting those communities has tremendous value for us and for others.

Two principles we will think about when investigating literary citizenship are reciprocity and usefulness. Reciprocity has to do with giving your time and expertise to your writing community in return for what that community has given you. Usefulness recognizes that your efforts to contribute to the community feel worthwhile.

132

My reading of *Howards End* resulted in one of the most important lessons of my life, and it came in the form of the book's famous epigraph, "Only connect..." Many, many writers have taken those words to heart over the years and, as I did, pinned them to a bulletin board or carried them in a wallet. Literary citizenship asks that you think about connections. How can you forge them or strengthen them? How can you make a difference?

> Literary citizenship refers to one's immersion in writing/reading communities near and far, physical and virtual, and recognizing the ways these communities benefit you. To be a good literary citizen, you in turn find ways of contributing to your communities—ways of giving back, being useful, and supporting those communities.

The poet Mary Oliver gives "Instructions for living a life: / Pay attention. / Be astonished. / Tell about it." A banner featuring these words hangs in my college's creative writing lounge. Every day, students and faculty walk beneath Oliver's words; every day, we reflect on why we are part of this writing community, and every day we participate in that community.

That's a good starting point for exploring literary citizenship, for although writing is often a solitary activity, it is also communal. The literary community (also called the writing community) is actually many communities linked by a love of writing and reading. It consists of a vast network of writers, readers, librarians, booksellers, agents, editors and publishers. All of us share the desire to promote reading and writing; our collective efforts to do this are called literary citizenship.

As students, one of the most immediate and accessible writing communities is the one made up of your classmates and teachers. If you're reading this book, you're probably already part of that kind of community. You're a member, but are you a citizen?

For our purposes, being a citizen means being an advocate. Advocates are individuals who seek out ways of supporting what they believe in. These can be quiet and private ways, or very public ways. The first step to practicing good literary citizenship is being on the lookout for ways you can contribute to making the world a better place for writers and readers. Those first steps will probably take place on and around your school grounds.

History

Long before anyone had heard of literary citizenship, writers united to talk about their work and share one another's work with the reading public. Literary salons, where writers met in one another's homes to talk about prose and poetry, were popular in France in the seventeenth and eighteenth centuries. What was important was conversation—the exchange of ideas in person and with conviction. Women often hosted salons, which were sometimes seen as alternatives to formal education.

Salons thrived in Britain as well as France; the Blue Stockings Society was a well-known salon founded by women around 1750 but including men, most notably Dr Samuel Johnson. Their emphasis was on culture and friendship, and the group influenced the way women were perceived and accepted as artists and thinkers. Much later, in the first half of the twentieth century, a group of English writers, artists and intellectuals began meeting in what would become perhaps the most well-known literary salon. Most of them lived in a part of London called Bloomsbury, and eventually the group became known as the Bloomsbury Group. Among the writers were Virginia Woolf and E.M. Forster, and most of the members came from upper-class society.

The Bloomsbury Group is associated with the 1920's, as are several other groups. Ernest Hemingway, James Joyce, F. Scott Fitzgerald, Gertrude Stein and Ezra Pound were among the British and American writers who met regularly at Shakespeare and Company, a Paris bookstore. And in New York City, writers Robert Benchley, Dorothy Parker, Alexander Woollcott, George S. Kaufman and Edna Ferber convened at the Algonquin Hotel; their group became known as the Algonquin Round Table.

On a much broader scale—one that included individuals immersed in writing, the arts, music, dance, drama and fashion—was the Harlem Renaissance. In the 1920's this movement supported African-American culture and challenged racism. James Weldon Johnson, Zora Neale Hurston, Langston Hughes, Jean Toomer and Alice Dunbar Nelson were among hundreds of writers and artists who left a legacy of deep cultural enrichment.

And in the 1960's writers Allen Ginsberg and Truman Capote met with artists Andy Warhol and Salvador Dali, and musicians Lou Reed and Bob Dylan. They convened in Warhol's studio, called The Factory, which became a center for experimental art.

These pockets of activity were identified with the cities in which they originated: London, Paris, New York... The work of the writers and artists involved received national and international acclaim. But it would be a mistake to

135

think that the work of creating and promoting literature was happening only in big cities or only among the privileged.

College campuses across North America were attracting and nurturing young writers and intellectuals. Creative writing programs began to flourish. Writing workshops—classes in which writers discuss and share their own work—became the first writing communities for many young people.

The Association of Writers & Writing Programs (AWP) was founded in 1967. This group of thirteen creative writing programs has grown into a collection of hundreds of colleges, universities, conferences and writing centers, all of which support writers and readers and help build audiences for literature. Their newsletter, the *Writer's Chronicle*, is a resource worth investigating, as is their annual writers' conference, which attracts writers and readers from around the world. (If your writing program is an AWP member program, they should receive seventy-five free copies of the *Chronicle* per month to distribute.)

By the 1980's, widespread computer access and growing familiarity with the internet allowed individuals worldwide to communicate quickly and efficiently. Writing communities expanded outward, beyond big cities, beyond college campuses. The word "community" broke the confines of physical places and came to include virtual, connected places and persons.

Online literary journals began to appear in the 1990's. These were initially dismissed by some writers as lacking prestige and being of lesser quality than print journals. The online literary journal movement spread rapidly, however, and the value of many of those journals became apparent. Today, there are numerous online journals that well-known writers publish in and support. Wherever your writing passion resides, you can find a literary journal that features it. Becoming acquainted with these journals, reading them, and possibly subscribing to them are acts of literary citizenship.

The rise of social media has also expanded our literary communities. Facebook makes it easy to keep track of or contact your favorite writers by *following* or *liking* their author pages or posting a message to their timelines. Worldwide, over a billion active monthly users are on Facebook. Twitter, created in 2006, has over 100 million users, including many writers who contribute to the 300 million tweets per day. Tweeting literary events and communicating with authors you admire via Twitter is another way to support the literary community.

Also in the 1990's, bookstores began adding cafes where readers could get coffee or tea and peruse books and magazines. Some writers flourish in these communal spaces and enjoy working there. The stimulation level— low-grade noise, the hum of background conversations— can be conducive to creating the sense of having both solitude and company.

With reference to cultural history, it's difficult to outline a clear or linear path leading to the birth of what is now called literary citizenship. But in the last decade a number of writers across the country have spoken in articulate and accessible ways about participating in the writing community. Their comments became sparks that lit the way for others to begin their own journey of literary citizenship.

One such writer was Cathy Day. In 2011 she made a blog post about literary citizenship. This is an abbreviated version of her remarks:

> I've been teaching creative writing for almost twenty years now, and here's something I've observed: what brings most people

to the creative writing classroom or the writing conference isn't simply the desire to "be a writer," but rather (or also) the desire to be a part of a literary community.

Deep down, we know that not everyone who signs up for the class or the conference will become a traditionally published writer. Well, so what?...

Lately, I've started thinking that maybe the reason I teach creative writing isn't just to create writers, but also to create a populace that cares about reading. There are many ways to lead a literary life, and I try to show my students simple ways that they can practice what I call "literary citizenship." I wish more aspiring writers would contribute to, not just expect things from, that world they want so much to be a part of.

Cathy Day included a list of suggestions on how you can become a good literary citizen—ways aspiring writers, like you, can give back and promote the importance of reading and the craft of writing. Many of those suggestions are included later in this chapter.

A very accessible resource, *The Write Crowd: Literary Citizenship & the Writing Life,* was published by Lori A. May in 2015. This affordable book, from Bloomsbury Publishing, outlines ways that writers and readers can participate in their literary communities. In her introduction, May writes: "Supporting and encouraging my fellow writers and contributing to their ambitions has not only made me feel involved as a literary citizen, but I have also experienced the side benefit of connecting on the most basic of human levels—and isn't that what art is meant to do? Through arts involvement, it's possible to not only feel a part of our geographic communities, but also, more importantly, experience that other definition of community—a sense of place and belonging among peers."

Reciprocity, usefulness, contribution, community: these are building blocks of the literary citizen's vocabulary.

First Steps

Now that you have some background on literary citizenship you can find ways to be useful to your writing communities. By doing so, you will begin to actually live your beliefs and dreams. Here's how you can take those first steps.

Before you can support the writing community, you have to be part of it. Perhaps you can start in a very small but important way: by saying hello. For writers, many of whom are introverts or accustomed to long periods of private reflection, speaking up can be a challenge. But the next time you have an opportunity to say hi, or to compliment a classmate on something s/he wrote, make that gesture. Instead of being one of the legions who take out a cell phone and tap at it until class starts, be the person who smiles or notices what someone else is reading. Sure, it's a risk to say hello. But guess what? It might actually go well. I met one of my best friends in graduate school by sending her an email saying I liked something she'd said in class. She complimented me back, and said she wanted to publish an essay of mine in a book she was editing. We're still good friends fifteen years later.

Maybe you're thinking that you're too shy to say hello. I'll let you off the hook for now; you don't have to approach anyone if you're not ready. But why not let your favorite writers know you admired something they've published? You can do so on Facebook or Twitter. It's quick and easy and it always makes the recipient feel great. Go to a writer's Facebook page and follow or like it and, if you're feeling brave, leave a quick post about what you appreciated about their work.

Here's another easy step: tell a friend about a book you enjoyed. That simple act—recommending a book—benefits the writing community in at least three ways. First, it allows you to share enthusiasm for reading. Second, it establishes or reinforces a personal connection, which is part of building community and being a citizen. Third, if the friend is actually in the market for a new read, s/he might purchase the book. That benefits the bookseller and the writer. In a way, a circle is formed. The author originally wrote the book in hopes, at least partially, that it would make an impression on a reader. You, as the reader, "repaid" that author by sharing your recommendation, which may result in another sale. That is a kind of reciprocity and it's how ripple effects happen—one person makes a decision to act, and that action affects somebody else who may, in turn, do the same thing. Remember: *only connect...*

Bigger Steps: Literary Citizenship Projects for Individuals and Groups

When you're ready to move on to new challenges, you might start by asking yourself what you're good at. Literary citizenship isn't supposed to hurt. It's a way of assessing your own skills and using them to add to the community.

The more you participate, the more ideas you will have about being part of your writing communities. Here are some ideas for what you can do:

GET YOUR FRIENDS TOGETHER AND CREATE A WRITING CHALLENGE

Perhaps everyone can write two pages per week, or a poem per week. Make it fun. If you want, you can have writing prompts or share your work online. This will keep everyone motivated and connected. *↖ gone?*

WRITE ABOUT AUTHORS AND BOOKS ON FACEBOOK, TWITTER OR OTHER SOCIAL MEDIA

If you're not sure what to write about, keep it simple: "Looking forward to _____'s new book!" or "I'm halfway through _____. I love it!"

START A DORM READING NIGHT *⏋*

For one hour a week, everybody reads in their rooms or in common spaces. Afterwards, get together and talk about your books and have some snacks. Or start a book/movie club, where everyone reads a book and then watches the movie adaptation.

first pear!

WRITE BOOK REVIEWS

There is an art to this, and you can learn it. Start by reading book reviews, which you can find in (online) newspapers and literary journals. Notice what kinds of things the reviewers include, such as a summary of the book, a sample of the author's writing style, and insightful commentary on the book's themes. When you're enthusiastic about a book you've read, try your own review and then share it by posting on your blog or on social media.

START A BLOG *Do you have blogs?*

Focus on an aspect of reading and/or writing that you care about, (for example, Why I Love YA Novels or 20 Contemporary Poetry Books for College Students). You can write about the most influential books of your childhood, or set up a challenge such as reading a book a

141

month and then writing about it. Blogs are good forums for creative, verbal individuals. There's no wrong way to be enthusiastic.

ATTEND POETRY OR OTHER READINGS

Stick around after the reading and tell the author(s) that you enjoyed their work. If you can afford to, buy their books!

SUPPORT INDEPENDENT BOOKSTORES

If you're lucky enough to have an independent bookstore in your community, attend their events, buy your books there, and encourage your friends to do the same.

READ TO YOUR LITTLE BROTHERS AND SISTERS/NIECES AND NEPHEWS

Buy them books for birthdays and holidays. Be a model for them so they begin to see that reading is cool and fun. Or have a craft day where you and the children in your life create book covers or movie posters for their favorite books.

BECOME A CONVERSATION PARTNER FOR AN ESOL STUDENT

You will help a student from another country learn English. And in turn, you will learn about a new culture. Or become a tutor in English or creative writing. Help someone else improve their writing and reading skills.

PARTICIPATE IN A WRITING CLUB ON CAMPUS

If none already exist, start one. My school has three, each with a different focus. Students get together and generate new work in one; in another they read their writing aloud and offer constructive criticism; and the third is for novelists who share their work over time.

SUBSCRIBE TO A LITERARY JOURNAL

If you're not sure how to find one, look at NewPages. com or search "literary journals." There are hundreds, so you might want to begin by reading samples online. Your local bookstore and/or campus library might carry some. This is especially important to those of you who want to someday publish your work in literary journals. They may eventually support you, so why not support them?

ORGANIZE A BOOK DRIVE FOR SOLDIERS OR FOR FLEDGLING COMMUNITY CENTERS OR LIBRARIES

Contact the organization and see what they need, then decide on the best way of collecting books. It might be as simple as asking your friends to drop off novels they've completed, or as extensive as placing receptacles around campus and publicizing the book drive. Sometimes starting small is a good idea, but if you're ready to go big, then go big!

CREATE LENDING LIBRARIES IN THE DORMS ON CAMPUS

Sure, your school probably has a library. But it can be really nice to just walk to the front desk in your pajamas and borrow a book.

THROW A BOOK-SWAP PARTY

Try something like a Book Cook-Out: everyone brings a book that they love to a barbecue. You eat, you talk about books, you swap and share those books. This is a great way to meet people, have fun, and share your love of reading and writing. Or for Halloween, have everyone dress as a character from a book and bring a scary novel to the party with them. You can, again, swap those books and have fun sharing your enthusiasm for writing and reading.

Buy Books

If you can afford it, purchase five books a year. If you can afford ten, buy ten. If you can afford twenty, buy twenty! Post photographs of your bookcase on social media. Share your love of reading with others.

Organize a Cash Mob for Your Local Independent Bookstore

This is a big event, although not difficult to plan. Here are some guidelines:

1. Find a local independent bookstore. This works best if you have an actual independently owned bookstore in easy driving distance. Not everyone is so lucky, but if you are, this can be fun.
2. Decide if you want the cash mob to be a surprise to the bookstore owners or if the proprietors might benefit from knowing about the event. In our case, the bookstore has a small staff and we had concerns that they might not be able to accommodate the rush of a few hundred patrons in a short period of time. We notified them so they could have sufficient staff on hand.
3. Decide on a time and date *at least* a month in advance. This gives you time to publicize the cash mob. We chose a two-hour block on a weeknight, scheduled so that townspeople could drop by the bookstore on their way home from work.
4. Create publicity materials. For our cash mob, a student in the class designed a flyer that was distributed primarily electronically, although we also posted flyers across campus.

5. Two weeks before the event, use Facebook, Twitter, other social media and email to let friends, colleagues, neighbors and family members know about the event. Briefly explain the premise: to encourage many people to support a particular local business, all meeting at a designated time and spending a little money to help keep that business viable. It doesn't matter whether you spend $5 or $50, the point is to contribute something so that the business—in this case, a beloved bookstore—can remain vibrant. We suggested that cash mob participants buy a book, and if they couldn't afford a book, then purchase a magazine, and if they couldn't afford a magazine, buy a postcard.

6. One week before the event, confirm details with the proprietors. See if they have any concerns, or suggestions that will help the cash mob run smoothly. There might be parking concerns, for example, or other problems you haven't anticipated. Remember, this event is to benefit *them*; make sure they are not going out of their way to accommodate *you*.

7. One or two days before the event, use social media to remind everyone of the time and place. This should be a short, fun notice: "Don't forget about the cash mob on Thursday! We'll see you at 4 p.m. on Bridge Street!"

8. On the day of the event, volunteer to give rides to friends or neighbors who may want to participate. On our campus, students publicized bus routes and schedules in addition to carpooling to the bookstore. Class members were at the bookstore at the start of the cash mob and were able to greet everyone who came into the store.

9. Browse and mingle and buy some books! When dozens (or hundreds) of like-minded individuals are in the same place, all of whom love the same thing—in this case, books—it's not difficult to strike up a conversation. You can do it—just smile and say hi.

10. During the event, keep your eyes open in case anyone needs help. Stand in line and carry a pile of books for somebody. Make a friendly recommendation about a book you enjoyed. Check in with the proprietors and make sure everything's running smoothly on their end.

Our cash mob was a huge success. Students learned how to coordinate and publicize a major public event. The bookstore sold books and other merchandise. Community ties were strengthened. And authors got their books into the hands of several hundred enthusiastic readers.

If you have a classroom of students who know how to use social media—and the great majority of students do—publicizing the cash mob takes little time. Twenty students' Facebook or Twitter posts can attract hundreds of participants. And even if the turnout is small, remember, you still will have attracted more customers than would have normally been shopping for books that day.

Last But Not Least

Being a literary citizen is a lifelong endeavor. It is also a creative one. You don't need to stick to the suggestions in this chapter. Discover your own ways of advocating for writers and readers. Find your own ways of making the world a better place for creative endeavors.

Remember to pay attention. Find ways to be useful. And connect.

About the Contributors

Mary Ann Cain
Mary Ann Cain is Professor of English at Indiana University–Purdue University Fort Wayne where she teaches rhetoric, fiction, creative nonfiction, and women's studies. Her books include *Revisioning Writers' Talk* (SUNY Press, 1995), *Composing Public Space: Teaching Writing in the Face of Private Interests* (with Michelle Comstock and Lil Brannon) (Heinemann, 2010), and a novel, *Down from Moonshine* (Thirteenth Moon Press, 2009). She has published on public space, critical praxis, and the composition-creative writing nexus as well as short fiction, nonfiction essays, and blurred genre publications. She is currently working on a book about Margaret T.G. Burroughs, artist, teacher, activist and founder of two arts institutions in Chicago.

Dianne Donnelly
Dianne Donnelly is the Assistant Dean of Research for the College of Arts & Sciences at the University of South Florida. In addition to her interests in research and scholarship, she is a creative writer and pedagogue who addresses the theory and pedagogy of creative writing. Donnelly is the editor of the popular collection *Does the Writing Workshop Still Work?* (2010), author of *The Emergence of Creative Writing Studies as an Academic Discipline* (2011) and co-editor with Graeme Harper of *Key Issues in Creative Writing* (2012). She is a frequent presenter at the creative writing pedagogy forums at the Conference on College Composition and Communication (CCCC) and the

Association of Writers & Writing Programs (AWP) and associate editor of *New Writing: The International Journal for the Practice and Theory of Creative Writing*.

Trent Hergenrader
Trent Hergenrader is an Assistant Professor in the Department of English at the Rochester Institute of Technology. His research bridges creative writing studies, digital pedagogy, and game-based learning in courses where students use online tools and role-playing game mechanics to collaboratively create fictional worlds. His short fiction has appeared in *Fantasy & Science Fiction*, *The Mammoth Book of Dieselpunk*, and *Best Horror of the Year #1*, among other places. He is co-editor of *Creative Writing in the Digital Age* and a senior editor for *The Journal of Creative Writing Studies*. For more, visit his website at trenthergenrader.com.

Anna Leahy
Anna Leahy's book *Constituents of Matter* won the Wick Poetry Prize, and her poems and essays appear in *Crab Orchard Review*, *Fifth Wednesday Journal*, *The Pinch*, *The Southern Review*, *The Weeklings*, and elsewhere. She edited *Power and Identity in the Creative Writing Classroom*, which launched the New Writing Viewpoints series. She teaches in the MFA and BFA programs at Chapman University, where she curates the Tabula Poetica reading series and edits the international journal *TAB*. See more at www.amleahy.com.

Tim Mayers
Tim Mayers is an associate professor of English at Millersville University, where he teaches courses in composition,

creative writing, and rhetoric. He is the author of *(Re) Writing Craft: Composition, Creative Writing, and the Future of English Studies.* He is also a published poet and his novel manuscript, *Intelligence Manifesto,* won the 2007 Paradigm Prize.

Travis Nicholson

Travis Nicholson is an instructor of creative writing and assistant director of the Center for Writing and Communication at the University of Arkansas at Monticello. He received an MFA in fiction from Wilkes University in 2014. Current scholarly pursuits include hybrid creative writing/composition pedagogy as well as research into publishing practices of young adult speculative fiction and screenplays. He has worked as managing editor for *River and South* literary magazine and on staff at *The Foliate Oak* online. Finally, he believes that writing is a collaborative endeavor, so go out and become part of the community.

Julie Platt

Julie Platt is a hybrid scholar who researches composition, professional writing, and creative writing studies. She holds graduate degrees in poetry from Ohio University and Bowling Green State University, and a PhD. in rhetoric and writing from Michigan State University. Her critical work, creative work, and reviews have appeared in such publications as *Computers and Composition, Kairos, Peitho, Moon City Review, Barn Owl Review,* and *Weave,* and she is the author of the poetry collection *In the Kingdom of My Familiar* (Hyacinth Girl Press, 2014). She is a founding board member of the Creative Writing Studies Organization (http://www.creativewritingstudies.org/), and co-edits the Digital, Multimodal, and Multimedia section of the Journal of Creative Writing Studies (http://scholarworks.rit. edu/jcws/). She is currently Assistant Professor of English at the University of Arkansas at Monticello.

Garry Craig Powell

Garry Craig Powell is an Englishman who was educated at the universities of Cambridge and Durham. (He also has an MFA from the University of Arizona.) He has lived in Portugal, Spain, Poland and the United Arab Emirates, where his debut collection of linked stories, *Stoning the Devil* (Skylight Press, 2012), is set. His fiction has appeared in *Best American Mystery Stories, McSweeney's, Nimrod,* and many other literary magazines. Powell has recently completed a historical novel about the Italian poet, playboy, soldier and statesman Gabriele D'Annunzio. He currently teaches creative writing at the University of Central Arkansas and contributes to *Rain Taxi*.

Joseph Rein

Joseph Rein is co-editor of *Creative Writing in the Digital Age* and *Dispatches from the Classroom*. His critical work has appeared in *Beyond the Workshop, New Writing,* and *The Writing Lab Newsletter.* His fiction has been nominated for a Pushcart Prize, and has appeared most recently in *Iron Horse Literary Review, The Pinch Literary Review*, and *Ruminate Magazine*. He is currently an Assistant Professor of Creative Writing at the University of Wisconsin-River Falls.

Donna Steiner

Donna Steiner's essays and poetry have been published in literary journals including *Fourth Genre, The Bellingham*

Review, The Sun, Full Grown People and *The Manifest Station*. She teaches literary citizenship and creative writing at the State University of New York in Oswego and is a contributing writer for *Hippocampus Magazine*. A chapbook of five essays, *Elements,* was released by Sweet Publications.

Stephanie Vanderslice

Stephanie Vanderslice's scholarly essays on the teaching of creative writing have been published nationally and internationally in such publications as *College English* (which she guest-edited with Kelly Ritter in 2008), *College Composition and Communication*, and *New Writing: An International Journal of Theory and Practice*. She has published three books: *Can It Really Be Taught?: Resisting Lore in Creative Writing Pedagogy* (Heinemann, 2007), *Teaching Creative Writing to Undergraduates: A Guide and Sourcebook* (Fountainhead, 2012) (both with Kelly Ritter) and *Rethinking Creative Writing* (Professional and Higher Partnership, 2012). Her fiction and nonfiction has appeared in many journals, anthologies and online publications and she is currently at work on a novel, *Beautiful, Fragile Things* and a memoir. In 2012 she was named Carnegie Foundation for the Advancement of Teaching US Professor of the Year for the state of Arkansas. She is Professor of Creative Writing and Director of the Arkansas Writers MFA Workshop at the University of Central Arkansas.

Bibliography

Useful websites

Association of Writers & Writing Programs, *Guide to Writing Programs* (https://www.awpwriter.org/guide/guide_writing_programs)

—— *Directory of Conferences & Centers* (https://www.awpwriter.org/wcc/directory_conferences_centers)

National Novel Writing Month, http://nanowrimo.org

Poets & Writers, http://www.pw.org

References

Andreasen, N. 2005, *The Creating Brain: The Neuroscience of Genius* (New York: Dana Press)

Atwood, M. 2012, "Why Wattpad Works," *The Guardian* (6 July 2012) http://www.theguardian.com/books/2012/jul/06/margaret-atwood-wattpad-online-writing

Bishop, W. 1997 (ed.), *Elements of Alternate Style* (Portsmouth, NH: Boynton/Cook)

Bishop, W. & D. Starkey 2006, *Keywords in Creative Writing* (Logan, UT: Utah State University Press)

Bolt, B. 2004, "The Exegesis and the Shock of the New," *TEXT Special Issue* 3, http://www.textjournal.com.au/speciss/issue3/bolt.htm

Carr, N. 2010, *The Shallows* (New York: W.W. Norton)

Cirillo, F. 2013, *The Pomodoro Technique* (Berlin: FC Garage GmbH)

Cross, K. & T. Angelo 1988, *Classroom Assessment Techniques: A Handbook for Faculty* (Ann Arbor, MI:

National Center for Research to Improve Postsecondary Teaching and Learning)

Day, C. 2011, "Literary Citizenship," *The Bird Sisters* ([web blog post] 9 March) http://thebirdsisters.blogspot. co.uk /2011/03/literary-citizenship-by-cathy-day.html

Edwards, B. 2012, *Drawing On the Right Side of the Brain* (New York: Tarcher)

Ferris Bueller's Day Off 1986, dir. John Hughes (Paramount Pictures)

Forster, E.M. 1989, *Howards End* (New York: Vintage International)

George, E. 2004, *Write Away: One Novelist's Approach to Fiction and the Writing Life* (New York: Perennial Currents)

Gladwell, M. 2008, "Late Bloomers: Why Do We Equate Genius with Precocity?" *The New Yorker* (20 October) http://www.newyorker.com/magazine/2008/10/20/ late-bloomers-2

Goldberg, N. 1986, *Writing Down the Bones: Freeing the Writer Within* (Boston: Shambala)

Grandin, T. 1996, *Thinking in Pictures: My Life with Autism* (New York: Vintage)

Guest, B. 2002, "Invisible Architecture," *Poetry Foundation* (15 Feb, 2010) http://www.poetryfoundation.org/ learning/essay/238690

Houston, P. 2009, "A Conversation with Toni Morrison," *O, The Oprah Magazine,* http://www.oprah.com/ omagazine/Toni-Morrison-on-Writing

Hugo, R. 1979, *The Triggering Town: Lectures and Essays on Poetry and Writing* (New York: W.W. Norton)

Irving, J. 2005, Interview, *The Daily Show with Jon Stewart* (Comedy Central, 17 August) http://thedailyshow. cc.com/videos/36k9p4/john-irving

Kealey, T. 2013, *The Creative Writing MFA Handbook: A Guide for Prospective Graduate Students*, second ed. rev. and updated (New York: Bloomsbury)

Keller, G. with J. Papasan 2013, *The ONE Thing: The Surprisingly Simple Truth Behind Extraordinary Results* (Austin, TX: Bard)

King, S. 2000, *On Writing: A Memoir of the Craft* (New York: Pocket Books)

Kinnett, D. 2014, "10 Things Not to Do at a Poetry Reading," *No Categories* ([web blog post] April 13) http://nocategories.net/ephemera/ten-things-literary-reading/

Klemm, W. 2013, "Why Writing By Hand Could Make You Smarter," *Psychology Today* (14 March) http://www.psychologytoday.com/blog/memory-medic/201303/why-writing-hand-could-make-you-smarter

Kleon, A. 2012, *Steal Like an Artist: 10 Things Nobody Told You about Being Creative* (New York: Workman)

Knoblauch, C. and L. Brannon 1984, *Rhetorical Traditions and the Teaching of Writing* (New Jersey: Boynton/Cook)

Koenig, J. 2013, "Sonder," *The Dictionary of Obscure Sorrows*, http://www.dictionaryofobscuresorrows.com/post/23536922667/sonder

Krauth, N. 2002, "The Preface as Exegesis," *TEXT* 6:1, http://www.textjournal.com.au/april02/krauth.htm

Kroll, J. 2004, "The Exegesis and the Gentle Reader/Writer," *TEXT Special Issue* 3, http://www.textjournal.com.au/speciss/issue3/kroll.htm

Lamott, A. 1994, *Bird by Bird: Some Instructions on Writing and Life* (New York: Anchor)

Leahy, A. 2013, "Yes and No," *Minerva Rising* ([web blog post] September 26) http://minervarising.com/contributors-blog-yes-and-no-by-anna-leahy/

May, J. 2013, "On Giving a Not Terrible Reading" *Poets & Writers* ([webblogpost]9September)http://www.pw.org/content/jamaal_may_on_giving_a_not_terrible_reading/

May, L. A. 2015, *The Write Crowd: Literary Citizenship & the Writing Life* (New York: Bloomsbury)

Mayers, T. 2005, *(Re)Writing Craft: Composition, Creative Writing, and the Future of English Studies* (Pittsburgh, PA: University of Pittsburgh Press)

McCarthy, C. 2007, Interview, *The Oprah Winfrey Show* ([video] 5 June) http://www.oprah.com/oprahsbookclub/Oprahs-Exclusive-Interview-with-Cormac- McCarthy-Video

Mosley, W. 2009, *This Year You Write Your Novel* (New York: Little, Brown, and Company)

Myers, D.G. 1996, *The Elephants Teach: Creative Writing Since 1880* (Englewood Cliffs, NJ: Prentice Hall)

Oates J. C. 2003, "Reading as a Writer: The Artist as Craftsman." *The Faith of a Writer: Life, Craft, Art* (New York: Ecco)

Oliver, M. 2008, *Red Bird* (Massachusetts: Beacon Press)

Patchett, A. 2013, *This Is the Story of a Happy Marriage* (New York: Harper)

Robinson, A. 2012, "How to Give a Poetry Reading," *Publishing Genius* ([web/feature] April 23) http://www.publishinggenius.com/?p=730

Rogers, E. 1997, "Stretch a Little and Get Limber: Warming Up to (and with) Grammar B," *Elements of Alternate Style*. Wendy Bishop (ed.), (Portsmouth, NH: Boynton/Cook)

Sommers, N. 1980, "Revision Strategies of Student Writers and Experienced Adult Writers," *College Composition and Communication* 31:4, 378–88.

Spitzer, M. 2014, "Pointers for Performance of Poetry and Prose," ([online video] 10 April) https://www.youtube.com/watch?v=9tgpQBwkqzk

Stafford, W. 1986, *You Must Revise your Life* (Ann Arbor, MI: University of Michigan Press)

Welch, N. 1997, *Getting Restless: Rethinking Revision in Writing Instruction* (Portsmouth, NH: Heinemann)

Index